Five Acts of Love

Abdul-Rahman Abdullah
Hoda Afshar
Megan Cope
Eugenia Flynn
D Harding
Saodat Ismailova
Khaled Sabsabi
Larissa Sansour
& Søren Lind
Yhonnie Scarce
Ali Tahayori
Hossein Valamanesh

Curated by Nur Shkembi

Australian Centre for
Contemporary Art
27 June – 24 August 2025

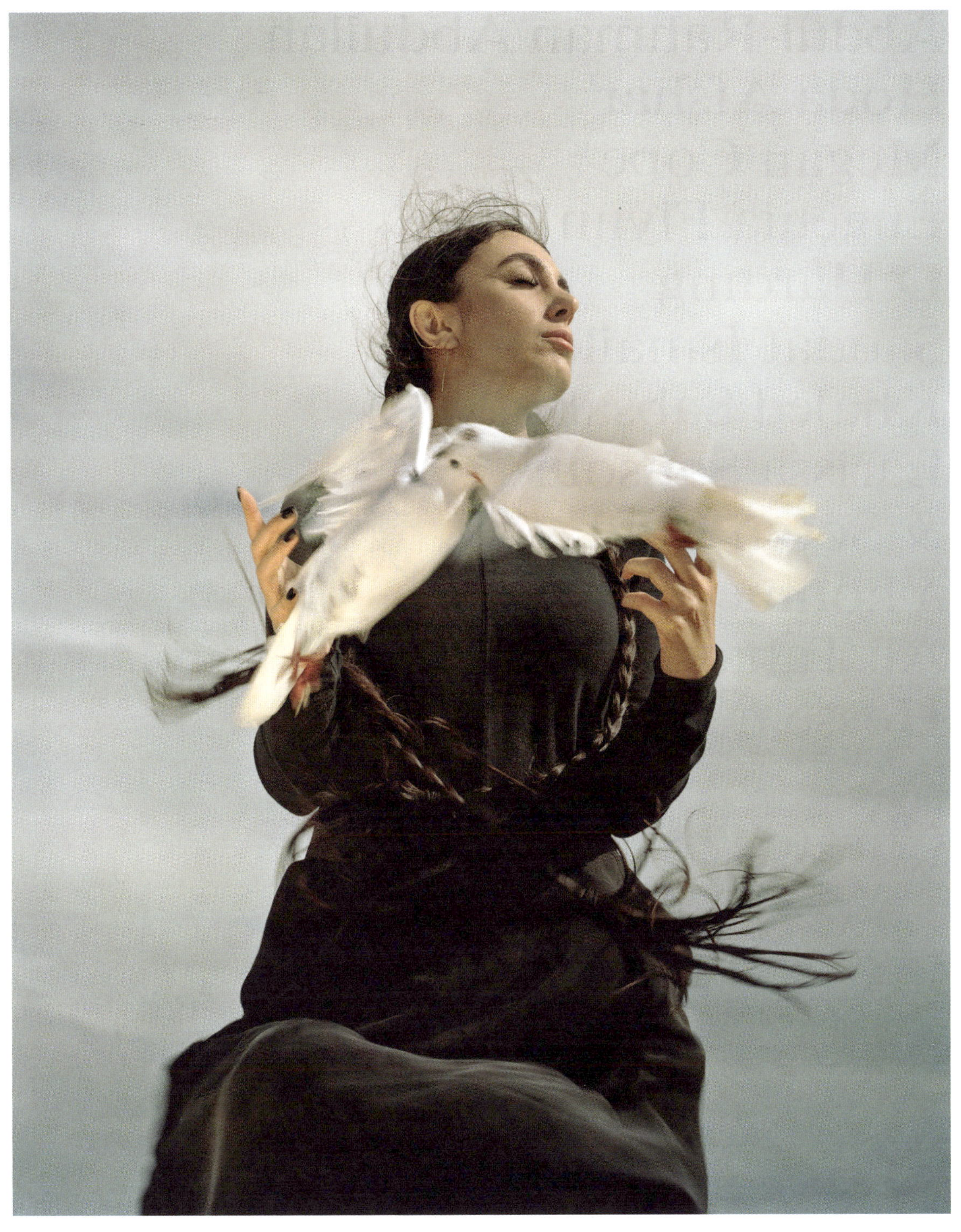

Hoda Afshar, *Untitled #7*, from *In turn* series 2023, framed photographic print, 165.0 x 132.0 cm. Courtesy the artist and Milani Gallery, Meanjin/Brisbane

ACCA acknowledges the Wurundjeri Woiwurrung peoples as sovereign custodians of the land on which we work and welcome visitors, along with the neighbouring Boonwurrung, Bunurong, and wider Kulin Nation. We acknowledge their longstanding and continuing care for Country, and we recognise First Peoples art and cultural practice has been thriving here for millennia. We extend our respect to ancestors and Elders past and present, and to all First Nations people.

Advisory note: This publication contains sensitive content. Reader discretion is advised. Selected texts and artworks reference subjects of suicide and genocide, and at times contain mature language.

Foreword

It is a great honour to present *Five Acts of Love* at the Australian Centre for Contemporary Art. Curated by the exceptional Dr Nur Shkembi OAM, the atmosphere of the exhibition holds a delicate balance of tenderness and strength, inviting pause, and the space to reflect on the vital importance of choosing love and tuning into our shared humanity.

Although defined, the five acts—resistance, revolution, intimacy, memory and *fanaa* (annihilation)—embrace the different expressions of love as interconnected, non-linear and complex. These acts of love are inextricably linked, a notion that is poetically shared through Nur's nuanced curation; creating an exhibition where connection is championed and complexity is not shied away from.

Five Acts of Love brings together the work of eleven artists and collectives: Abdul-Rahman Abdullah, Hoda Afshar, Megan Cope, Eugenia Flynn, D Harding, Saodat Ismailova, Khaled Sabsabi, Larissa Sansour & Søren Lind, Yhonnie Scarce, Ali Tahayori, and Hossein Valamanesh. Together their work stands as a contemporary reflection of our times, a testament to my belief that art can illuminate our path through darkness.

We are deeply grateful to the resilience and creativity shown by this outstanding group of artists, and to Nur's thoughtful, rigorous, and ambitious curation. The heart of *Five Acts of Love* is so beautifully laid out in Nur's curatorial essay, which echoes the flow of the exhibition and offers her reading of how selected works speak to one, multiple, or all of the acts of love.

I would like to also extend sincere thanks to former ACCA Artistic Director and CEO, Max Delany, for engaging Nur over a year before the exhibition's opening—it has been an honour to step into the role with this exhibition underway. Equally, it has been a pleasure

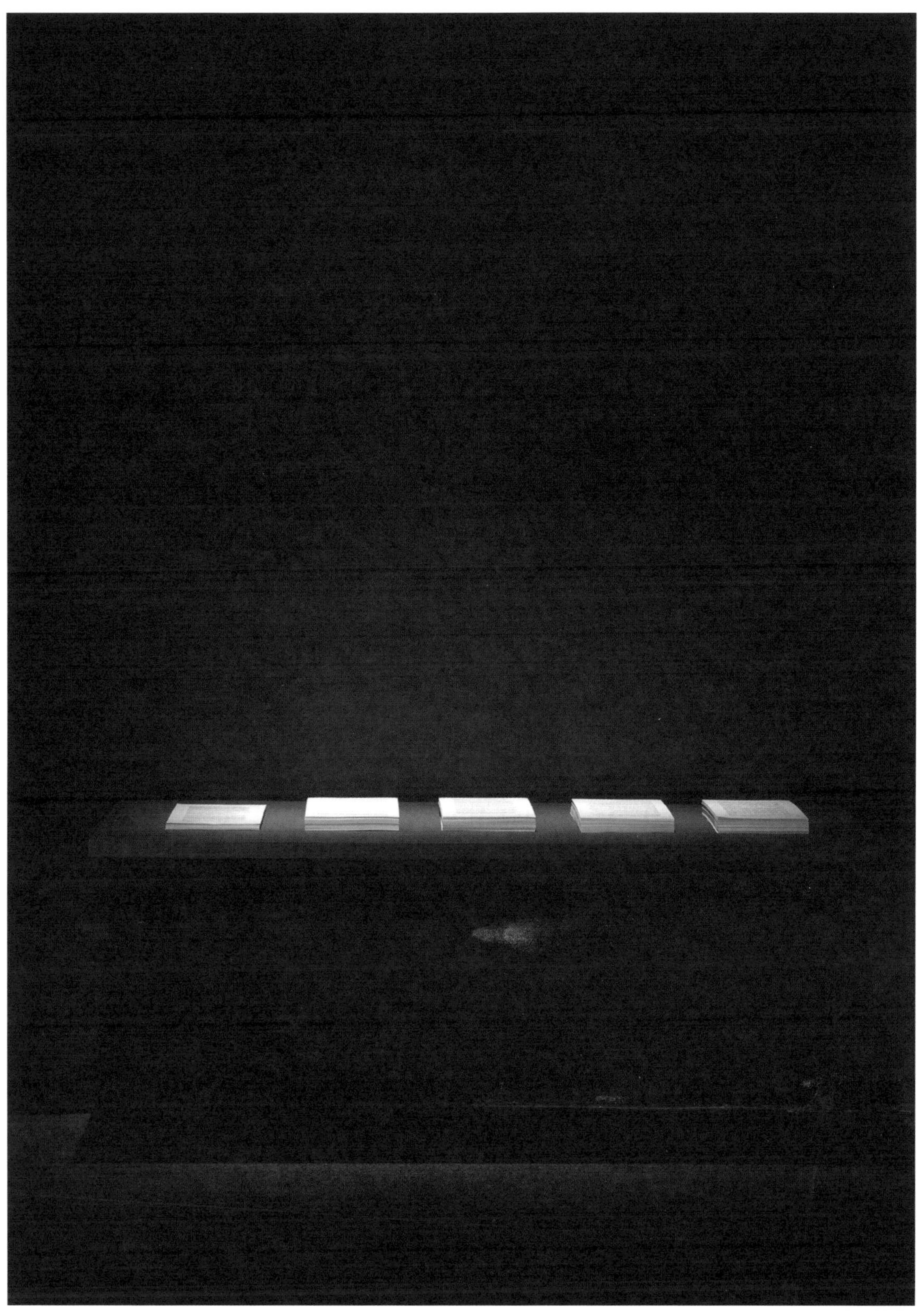

Khaled Sabsabi, *At the speed of light* (detail) 2016, 11 channel HD video sculpture installation, audio, 25.0 x 4.0 cm gold leaf / acrylic and enamel paint work on photographic paper, 5 multilingual text panels on paper. Courtesy the artist and Milani Gallery, Meanjin/Brisbane

to observe, support and work with the exhibition's coordinating curators Dr Jessica Clark and Dr Shelley McSpedden, who have continued to demonstrate the utmost care and consideration for the people, ideas and works that make up *Five Acts of Love*. And further thanks to ACCA Curator, Sophie Prince, who has been a great support and for leading the production of the exhibition catalogue.

We extend our appreciation to the catalogue contributors. Jessica Clark's text on love as resistance conjures stirring images of how and where one might observe, embody, or practice this form of love—a love that she so astutely describes as 'the strength within and collective action'. While Eugenia Flynn's contribution to *Five Acts of Love* spans her textual work within the exhibition and reflective text for the catalogue that together invoke love as revolution. Elyas Alavi's moving poetic and illustrative responses to the act of memory are an emotive counterpoint to the candor of Sara M Saleh's *A Dictionary of Intimacy*, and Dr Safdar Ahmed's compelling analysis of the notion of *fanaa* (annihilation). The scope of new commissions presented in this book purposefully extends the experience of the exhibition itself.

The exhibition would not have been realised without the commitment and support of Exhibition Partner Dulux, Government Partners, Creative Australia, Creative Victoria and City of Melbourne, as well ACCA's truly inspiring community of loyal donors. We also deeply value the support of our Media Partners 3RRR, Art Guide, Broadsheet and VAULT Magazine for their amplification of ACCA's important program. This multifaceted and visionary support of ACCA's operations is vital to platforming art that is *always New, always Now, always Free*.

In this divisive moment, *Five Acts of Love* reminds us that love is not only an emotional experience, but a powerful site of resistance and regeneration—a connecting force that can overcome those who seek to divide us. Exhibiting artists—and art more broadly—offer unique perspectives that, if let into our heart, may resonate profoundly, allowing us to navigate the complexities of our world through a lens of compassion and understanding.

Myles Russell-Cook
Artistic Director & CEO

Five Acts of Love
Dr Nur Shkembi

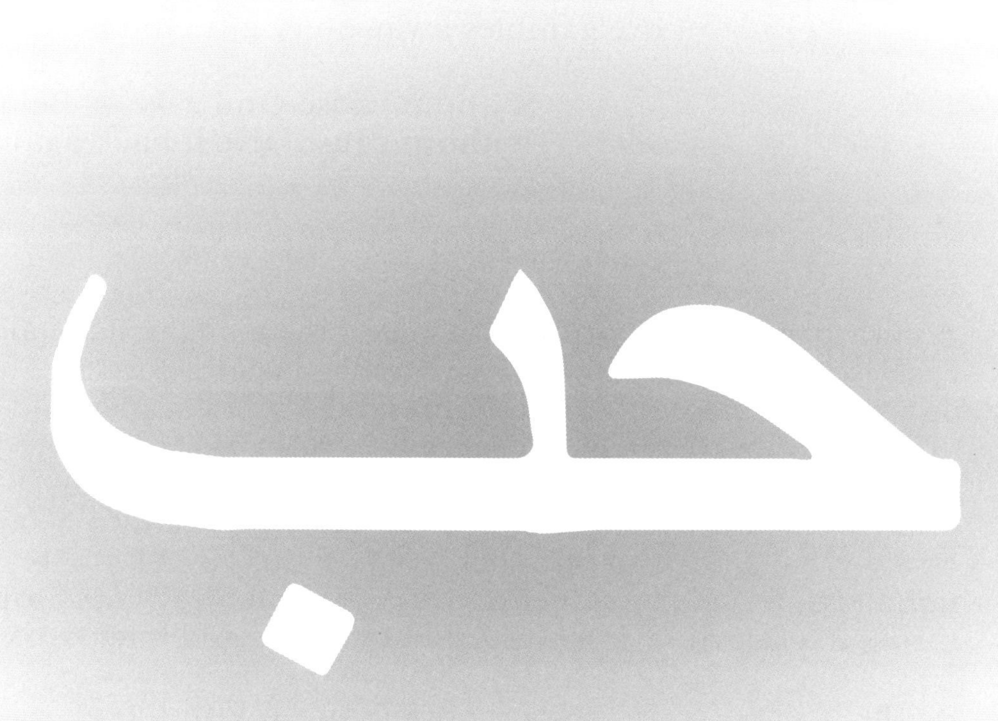

Love is reckless, not reason.
Reason seeks a profit.
Love comes on strong, consuming herself, unabashed.

Yet, in the midst of suffering,
Love proceeds like a millstone,
hard-surfaced and straightforward.

Having died to self-interest,
she risks everything and asks for nothing.
Love gambles away every gift God bestows.

Without cause God gave us Being;
without cause, give it back again.[1]

A curatorial essay is ordinarily meant to be an intellectual exercise of sorts, centred around a theme, embedded in an objective piece of research, presented as an academic offering, or even as a clever piece of writing (loosely disguising curatorial pontification). But for love, I really don't want to write an essay that is trying too hard to be an essay. What I hope to offer here and, in this exhibition, is not a lesson on love, rather a meditation on love *beyond* love through a selection of extraordinary artists and their work.

At the heart of *Five Acts of Love* is an exploration of love's unexpected and nuanced manifestations, an intrinsic action that can harness the utmost depth of our humanity in lieu of pop culture references to romance and kitsch images of love. The works are presented as a rumination on love as loss, as conversations about grief and yearning; of love presented as memory and memorialisation; of love as resistance and revolution, reimagined through continued connections to earth and sea; and love as intimacy, such as the intimacy found within the gentleness of familial gatherings, and in the company of comrades. Love is also present in the human register that tunes into the spiritual, and the total surrender that encompasses love of the Divine.

Love is a universal aspiration, wondrous, elusive, and for the most part, utterly tantalising. Yet, I write this from Australia, where First Nations communities have been massacred and dispossessed of their ancestral lands. I write from a place of grief, witnessing genocide in Gaza and mass deaths in the Democratic Republic of the Congo, Syria, Yemen, and many other locations around the world. In the face of such suffering, I feel the deterioration of our shared humanity. Amid this despair, I find only one place to return: love.

These five acts—resistance, revolution, intimacy, memory and annihilation (fanaa)[2]—are not linear or siloed. One act does not advance the other, instead they sit amongst each other, perhaps even in awe of one another. As such, artworks do not fit neatly into one of the five acts, nor are the artists prescribed to represent a distinct thematic. Rather, in this state of despair, it is fitting that the artists' works do not attempt to instruct or illustrate these ideas, but instead complicate and converse with them.

Each act of love circles around what we ultimately relinquish when we love and are loved. This is poignantly experienced within the installation *The lover circles his own heart* 1993 (Paris edition 2017) by the late Hossein Valamanesh. A delicate silk funnel, rotating endlessly on a motorized axis, evokes the spiritual meditative worship, practiced by the Mevlevi Sufi Order, called *sema*.[3] The work has become an iconic, legacy work by Valamanesh—who has been an influential figure for many diaspora artists—encapsulating the artist's extraordinary inner visual language. The circular or 'whirling' nature of the haptic sculpture gently compels the viewer to venture both closer and inwards. The work also includes a poem by thirteenth century Islamic scholar Jalāl ad-Dīn Muhammad Balkhī (commonly known in the West as the poet Rumi).

We came whirling
Out of nothingness
Scattering stars
Like dust
It sunders
All attachments
Every atom
Turns bewildered
Beggars circle tables
Dogs circle carrion
The lover circles his own heart.[4]

Valamanesh's work often ruminates on the messaging and poetics of Sufi philosophy, however, for this work the artist draws on the notion of the interconnectedness of humanity through the shared passing of time. Reflecting on the poem he stated:

> The poetry describes how everything is in perpetual motion: every atom turns bewildered, every star going around the earth moves, and, in that sense, the idea of change and time passing is very much part of that concept. And I feel that this is the way we are connected together, that we are not alone in this madness.[5]

For the artist, the visual likeness of a dervish in meditative *sema* also encompasses the spinning motion and circular aesthetic of the atom—the centre of all life. These revolutions set the scene for one of the ultimate forms of love, *fanaa*. In Sufism, it is said that the methodical whirling and circling enables spiritual clarity. The *semazen* describes:

> It is scientifically recognised that the fundamental condition of our existence is to revolve. There is no being or object which does not revolve, because all beings are comprised of revolving electrons, protons, and neutrons in atoms. Everything revolves, and the human being lives by means of the revolution of these

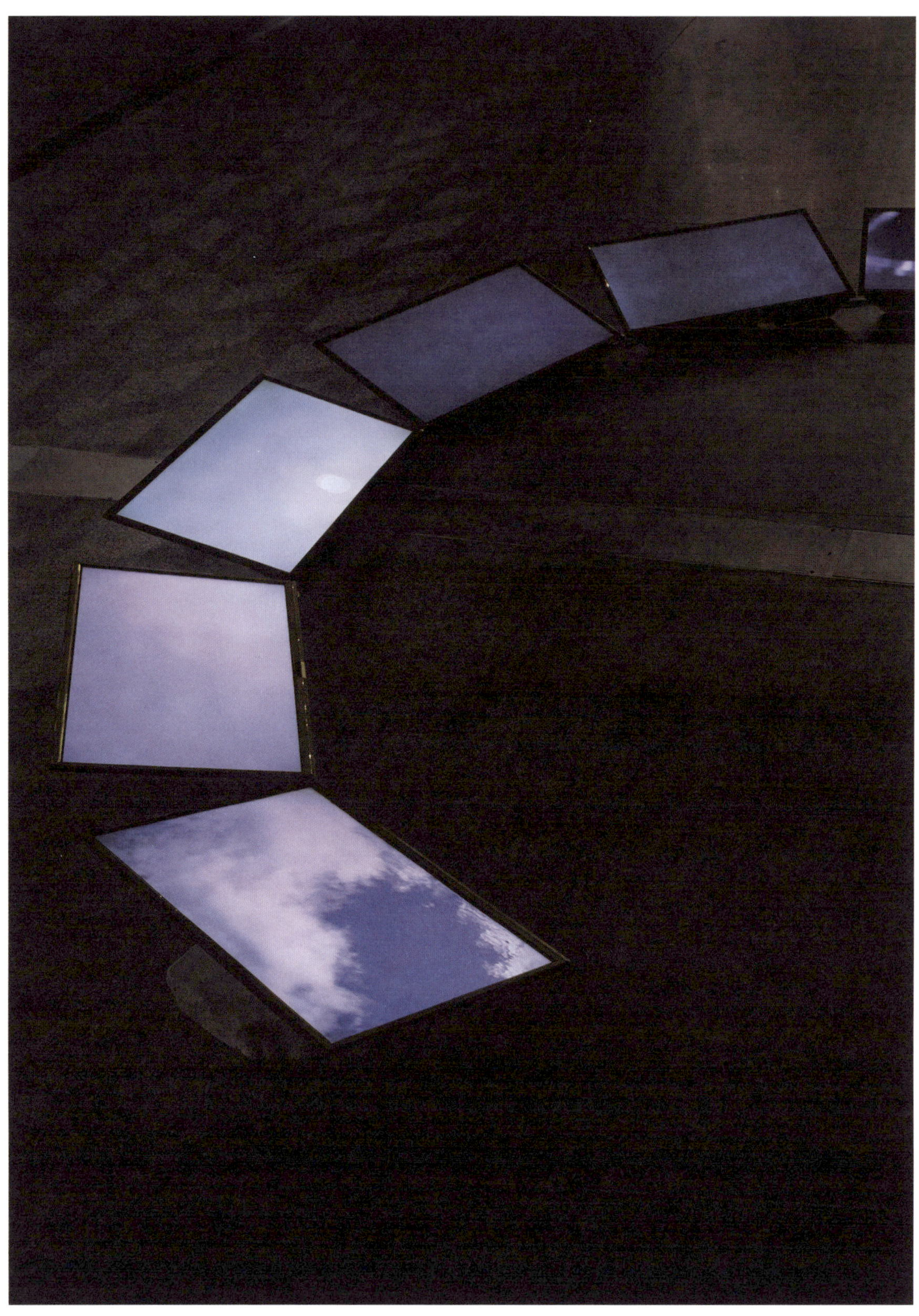

Khaled Sabsabi, *At the speed of light* (detail) 2016, 11 channel HD video sculpture installation, audio, 25.0 x 4.0 cm gold leaf / acrylic and enamel paint work on photographic paper, 5 multilingual text panels on paper. Courtesy the artist and Milani Gallery, Meanjin/Brisbane

> particles, by the revolution of the blood in his body, and by the revolution of the stages of his life, by his coming from the earth and his returning to it.[6]

Valamanesh's work is shown in conversation with Khaled Sabsabi's ethereal video installation, *At the speed of light* 2016. For Sabsabi, this work is a personal, spiritual and artistic exploration 'that considers science, philosophy and art in the modern digital era'.[7] Sabsabi reflects on *Nur*, or divine light, as both spiritual presence and a philosophical question:

> In Sufism (*tasawwuf*), it is very difficult to explain the true meaning of the Arabic word *Nur*. In Sufi text, the Divine describes Itself as being *Nur* and Divine mysteries become readily apparent through the *Nur* of knowledge. In the Qur'an it is also taught that 'Light is the purest entity that exists' and that there are different realms and worlds around us, with each realm having a functional and sustainable existence.[8]

Sabsabi goes on to reference one of the tenants of belief for Muslims, that being the existence of Angels who are created from light, and the unseen realm.[9] He reflects:

> Having considered these teachings and the scientific fact that physical light has limitations posed by its physical nature, and its dependence on energy, space and time; I propose the question, 'if we are able to travel at the speed of light, will we be able to enter and interact with the unseen realms?'[10]

The circular configuration of *At the speed of light* harmonises the physical and metaphysical nature of the light journey and gently points back to the hermetic connection at the core of all human existence—the atom. The beauty and majesty of witnessing *At the speed of light*, may also be accessed through actively understanding and receiving the sincere quest undertaken by the artist and his vulnerability in sharing it. Offered is a humble proposition to grapple with the notion of letting go of one's ego.

***

Ali Tahayori shares his yearning for intimacy in his series, *Archive of longing* 2024–25, which delicately portrays 'glimpses of love and longing reflected' within a familial history entangled in the political milieu of pre-and post-revolutionary Iran.[11] Using traditional Persian glass cutting techniques and geometric patterns known as Āine-Kāri aine, Tahayori reclaims family photographs once filtered through his mother's narrative, to now recast them through a queer diasporic lens. Tahayori states, 'revisiting these images after thirty years, I started seeing numerous possibilities, affiliations, and connections not included in my mother's original narrative. I began to tell my story with them'.[12] In the work we see printed glass that has been broken and reassembled, creating mirrored relief-like sculptural forms which Tahayori describes as a search for 'glimpses of intimacy and desire within a violent socio-political context'.[13] By approaching the archive from his lived experience, Tahayori layers together personal histories, intimacy and memory in his highly skilled and contemporary rendering of Āine-Kāri aine.[14]

Encountering love through the auspices of familial memory is also found within Abdul-Rahman Abdullah's *Pretty Beach* 2019, a monumental installation of wood and shimmering crystals. Abdullah recalls:

> I remember standing out on the jetty [at Pretty Beach in New South Wales] as a kid watching a fever of stingrays glide beneath me, tracing arcs through the shallow water. The rain drifted in like a soft curtain drawing across the bay, obliterating the rays from view as the surface of the water crumpled above them. I ran inside.[15]

The work is an exquisite meditation on grief and remembering. It responds to Abdullah's solemn childhood recollection of the death of Grandpa Cliffy, his paternal grandfather who died by suicide. Abdullah remembers receiving the news of his grandfather's death after years of cancer and diabetes ravaging his body: 'when his leg went, he dragged himself into his 1963 EH Holden, hooked up the exhaust and faded into sleep...he died holding pictures of us kids and letters we'd written. I hadn't visited Pretty Beach for many years, and then he was gone'.[16] Through this work Abdullah takes the opportunity to describe the resilience and fierce independence of his grandfather, a man who was respected amongst his peers at Paddy's Market where he was known as 'Honest Cliff'.[17] What Abdullah reveals in this profoundly beautiful work, is the malleability of memory, the complexity of familial histories, and the distance between love and loss as something both excruciatingly near and far.

***

In *Familiar Phantoms* 2023, Palestinian artist Larissa Sansour also explores memory—both the inherited and the lived, and as it pertains to identity. Produced in collaboration with long-time partner Søren Lind, the film blurs fiction and autobiography. Shot in a dilapidated mansion and interwoven with personal photos and Super 8 footage, it continues a key direction of Sansour's practice that 'often uses science fiction to address social and political issues' with the 'dialectics between myth, documentary and historical narrative', described by the artist as being central to her work.[18] The film's location 'serves as the seat of memory' and within the individual rooms 'vignettes are played out, adding a theatrical dimension, enlarging and exaggerating the narrative components, just as memory perpetually reworks, reinforces, adds and subtracts'.[19] The images are anchored by the consistent and soothing tone of the narrator, and as the film moves from one scene to the next, editing mimics the mechanics of memory, untangling and reassembling the deeply personal recollections of Sansour's childhood in Bethlehem.[20]

Love as memory and resistance is also held within Yhonnie Scarce's compelling photographic portrait installation *N0000, N2359, N2351, N2402* 2014. The installation

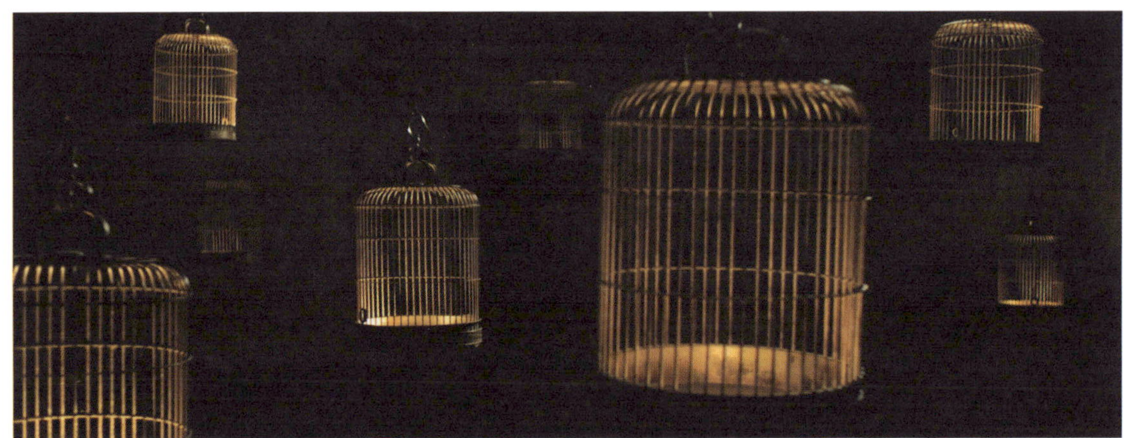

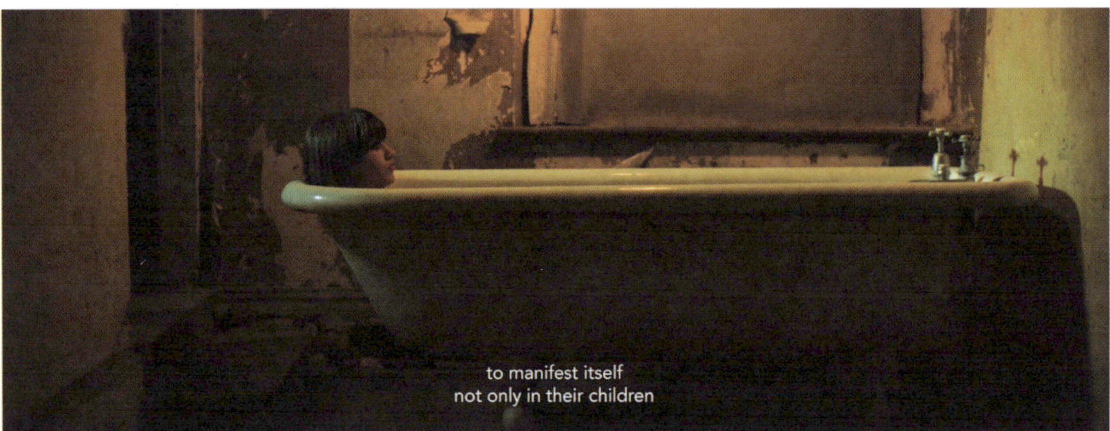

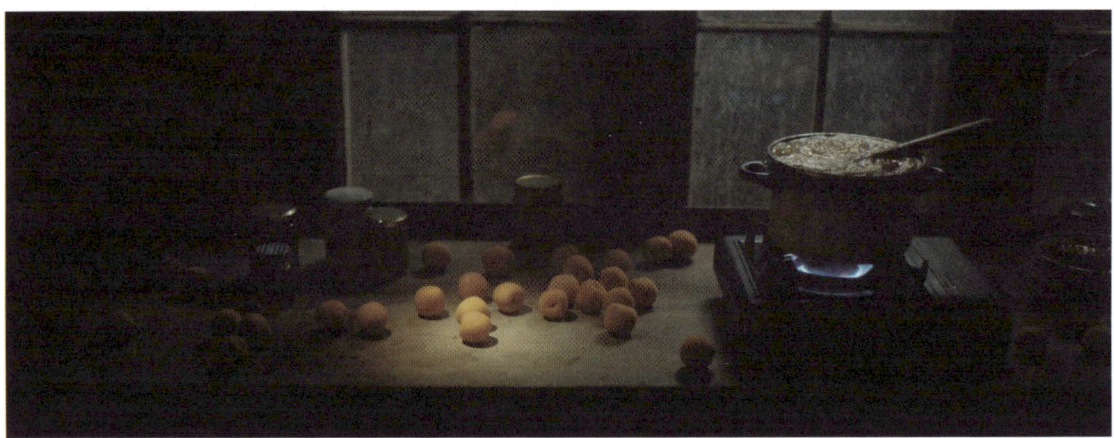

All images: Larissa Sansour & Søren Lind, *Familiar Phantoms* (still) 2023, Film, 42:00 mins. Courtesy the artists
Opposite page, all images: Soadat Ismailova, *Her right* (still) 2020, HD Video, 14:00 mins. Supported by Video Jam, UK. Courtesy the artist

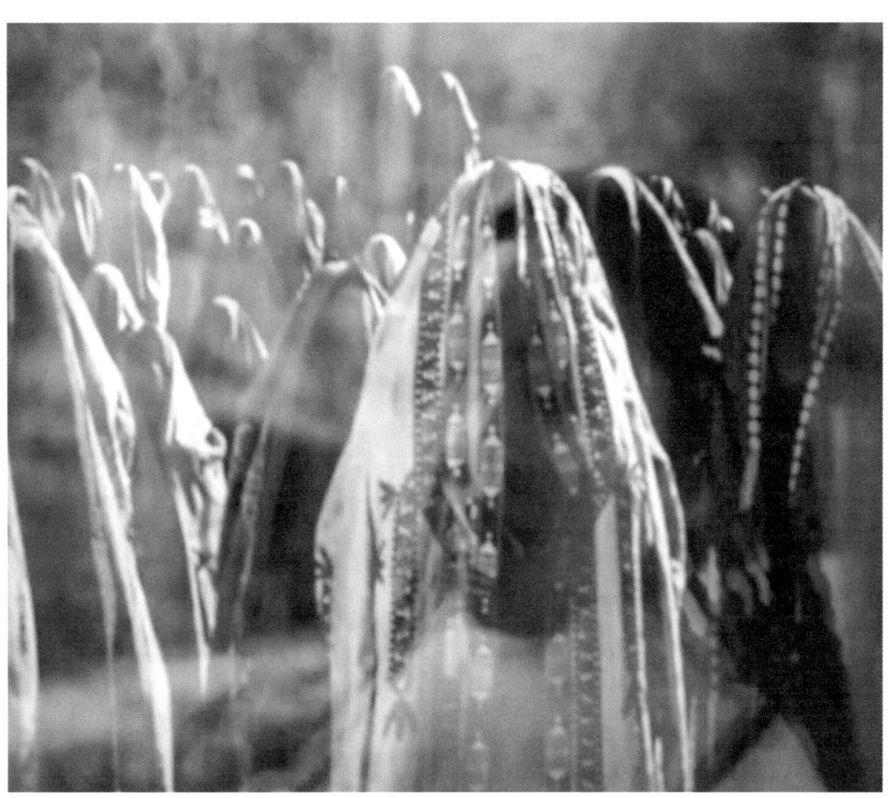

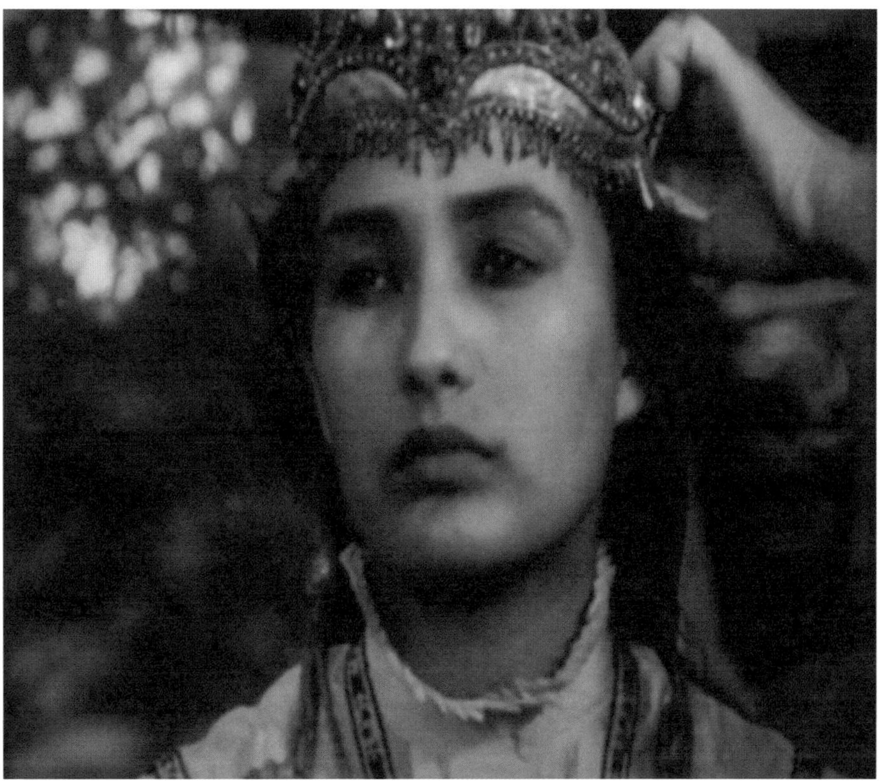

comprises of blown glass with a 'cracked and fractured finish' and a set of Scarce's archival family photographs presented to the effect of a natural history museum-style display.[21] Scarce describes the images of her ancestors as being 'displayed like specimens under bell-jars', a striking visual connotation to the period before the 1967 Referendum when Australia's First People were not recognised as part of the census, but instead were classified under the Commonwealth Government's Flora and Fauna Act.The artist's intensive archival research and dedication to truth telling can be seen in Scarce's coded handling of her chosen materials—here we observe the fragility of the glass belying the human resilience it contains. She comments:

> The first bell-jar contains blown glass Indigenous fruit. This outlines the comparison between flora and Indigenous peoples and how they once held a shared place in the white Australian conscience. The cracked finish of the bell-jars makes it hard to see the entire photograph clearly, this references the recording of Aboriginal history since colonial settlement, the truth of which is fractured and not all disclosed.[22]

Presented in dialogue, Sansour and Scarce's works share deeply personal histories, compelled by familial memory and the multiple lived realities of Indigenous people both in Australia and in Palestine. Abdullah's meticulously handcrafted gazelle, titled *Witness* 2025, quietly watches over their work in this same space. There is a palpable gentle quality to this sculpture that captures the innocence of this sublime creature, yet there is also a slightly uncomfortable ambiguity to the work. The gazelle's gaze posits, are we watching or are we the ones being watched?

***

D Harding's diptych *She come from the low-country, he come from the high-country II* 2025, unites Bidjara and Ghungalu soil across two panels. The almost four-metre-long diptych consists of Ghungalu red soil and acrylic binder on the left panel and the right panel Bidjara red soil and acrylic binder, honouring the intricacy and persistent knowledge held by the land. Harding notes:

> So when we can identify each shade of red by eye, and know where it came from, and know the process that I used to make the painting—that involves scale and sequence and distance—then we could speak for hours about how this is a painting about grandparents, and genealogy and land rights and language group inheritance, and how Nanna upheld some of her Bidjara roles even though she was Ghungalu, living away from Country in diaspora on Darumbal.[23]

Beyond the meticulous understanding of each pigment which Harding has collected and applied to each of the canvasses, there is another story held deeply within their work:

> At some point I must stop telling the life stories of my Elders, and inhabit my own experiences as a queer person—these two panels were conceived as a contained space that I have claimed for myself, where I live my Murri culture among the contemporary effects of colonial oppression in Central Queensland. Homophobia and misogyny are not ours—these two reds and their stories are my inheritance.
>
> "Don't look for figuration (for meaning), or for composition".[24]

Harding addresses the long-standing issues about who and how one loves, speaking to the misogyny and homophobia persisting in society across cultures and generations. Through his reflection on Country and communities and time, Harding raises questions about who has agency to truly be in the present.

Megan Cope invites us to witness the endurance of love through her work *The tide waits for no-one* 2020–21, by recalling stories of land and sea. The striking circular formation of glass, bone and mineral salt draws on natural elements to speak to the complex colonial history of Minjerribah (North Stradbroke Island), and Cope's practicing of colonial resistance through the maintenance and persistence of First Nation's knowledge. The work reveals the history of 'early colonisation of Quandamooka Country, where the hunting of Dugong and industrial scale processing became a lucrative marketplace'.[25] Cope explains that the installation references 'evidence of that now-banned industry—old glassware and brittle bones—can be found across the island's landscape, particularly in eroding dunes'.[26] The artist further contextualises the work describing the extraction and consumption of natural resources by colonisers:

> Between 1847 and 1969 the commercial processing of oil, bones, hides and meat occurred with very little regard of sustainability, rather Europeans arrived with the perception of 'Bounteous Seas' and very little recognition of the sophisticated land and sea management systems upheld by the Quandamooka Peoples.[27]

Cope's work subverts the colonial mark by reminding us of the continued resistance of nature as a regenerative force. Through her practice, Cope not only fiercely critiques the past but also nourishes the future.

In her poem *for love of country* 2025, Eugenia Flynn also addresses the implications of social and political colonial constructs, specifically the weaponisation of 'country' to justify violence. Flynn takes aim at the patriotic use of the phrase 'for love of country', seeking to break apart its racist and xenophobic power.[28] Flynn deduces 'Love is a power that can manifest in both good and bad ways'.[29] She arrives at this observation when reflecting on the incident in Melbourne at the 2025 ANZAC Day dawn service, when several attendees publicly heckled and booed the Welcome to Country address being delivered by Bunurong and Gunditjmara man Uncle Mark Brown. The racially charged aggression by the group of extremists, subsequently led to the withdrawal of a Welcome to Country at an ANZAC Day rugby match. Flynn regarding the recent events as ‘stark reminders of how love (of country) can be a negative force in Australian society’.[30] Flynn’s poem offers a potent reminder of the truth that love can be both a positive and negative force. But we are guided to an even higher understanding that love as resistance to racism and xenophobia is at the heart of what is good, not only for our ‘country’, but also for our humanity. *for love of country* anchors the subtle lines that permeate this exhibition—love is complex, confounding, and at times contradictory.

***

Saodat Ismailova’s hauntingly beautiful video essay *Her right* 2020, presents a flow of images of women in post-Soviet Uzbekistan. Compiled as a ‘film collage’ Ismailova describes the work as ‘created from Uzbek fiction and documentary films from 1927 to 1985, focusing on *Khujum*—the communist campaign that started at 1928 to emancipate women in Uzbekistan’.[31] Ismailova goes on to further contextualise the work:

> The film deploys a moment in the history when women found themselves flattened in-between traditional society and an imposed state ideology, risking their lives. Both veiled and unveiled women feared harassment—the veiled by the new regime, the unveiled by traditionalists. The women’s emancipation remained a major subject for Uzbek Soviet cinema.[32]

Her right is an ode or ‘love letter’ of sorts to the resilience of Ismailova’s film heroines. The opening of the film includes a solemn dedication in old Uzbek (which is written in the Arabic alphabet), that translates to: ‘The film is dedicated to the memory of women who sacrificed their lives for the freedom of Uzbek women today’.[33]

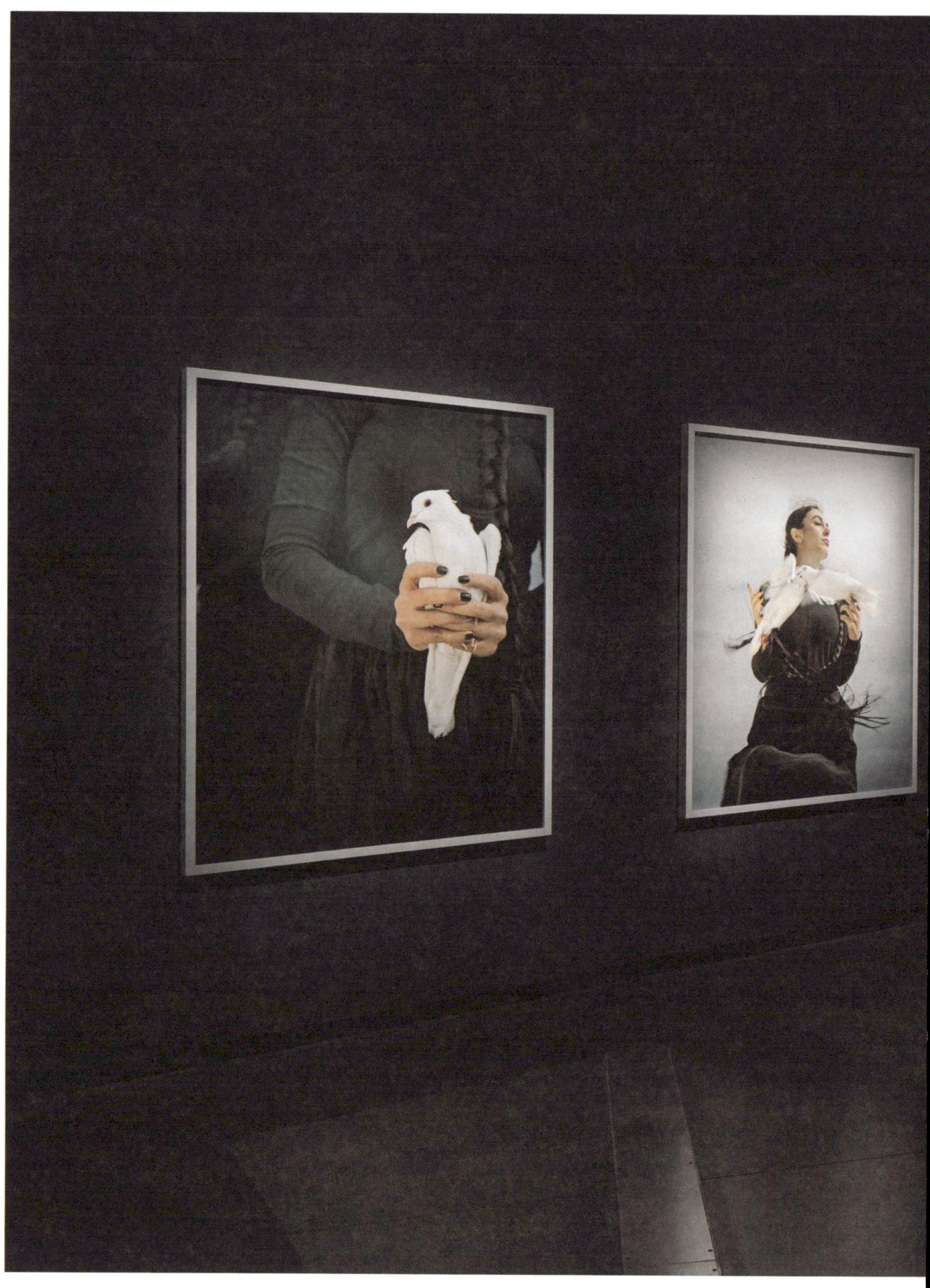

(L-R) Hoda Afshar, *Untitled #5*, *#7*, *#1*, #3, *#6* from *In turn* series 2023, framed photographic print, 165.0 x 132.0 cm. Courtesy the artist and Milani Gallery, Meanjin/Brisbane

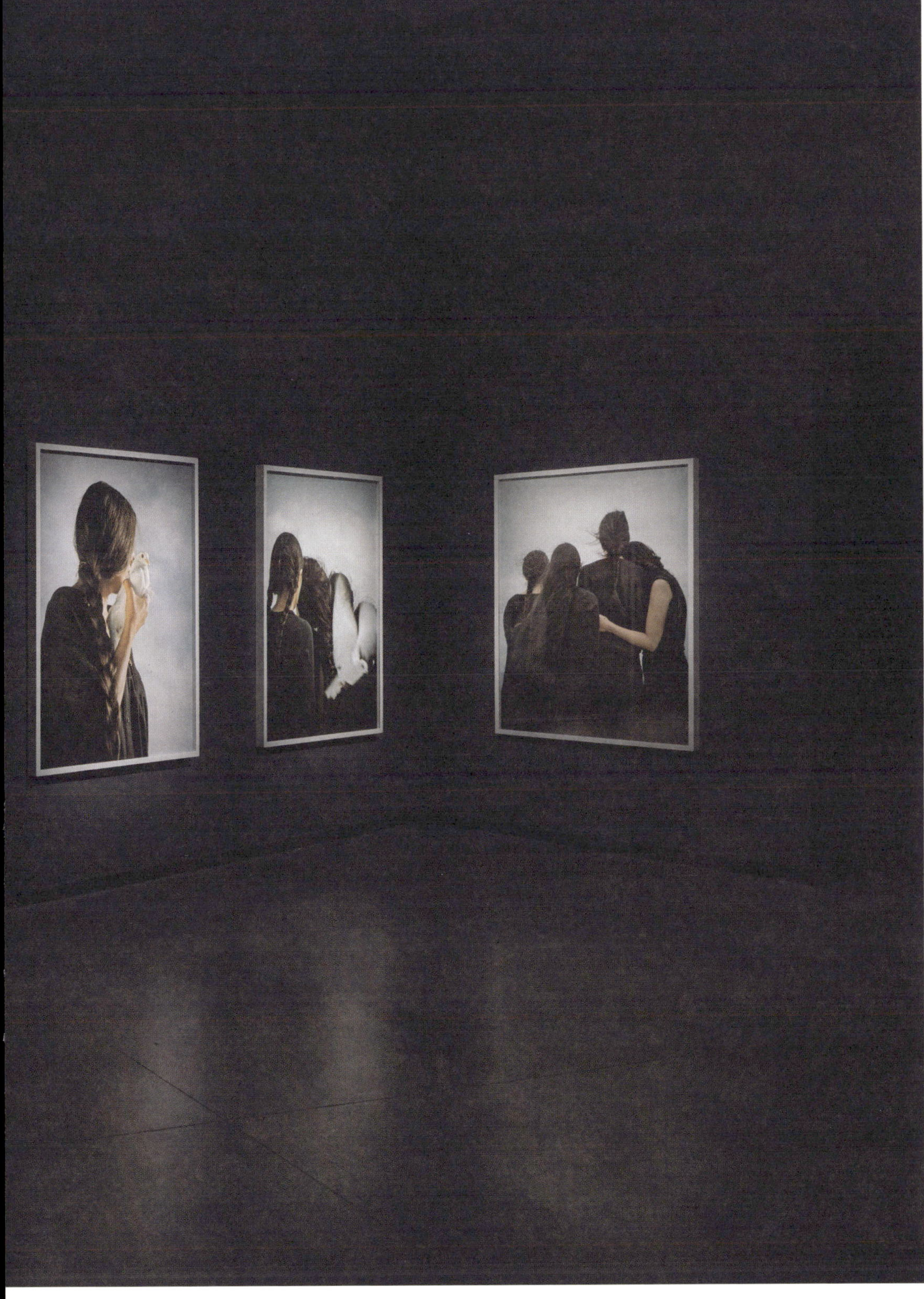

Striking imagery of the female body as a site of power is also seen in Hoda Afshar's luxurious portrait series *In turn* 2023. The series depicts women coming together in moments of intimacy and care, as a 'tribute and a testament to collective action and collective grief'.[34] Here, Afshar shares with us a vision: a prequel to a revolution through the intimate act of love in women braiding one another's hair. Afshar describes the staged series as being anchored by reality in portraying 'a practice common among Kurdish female fighters who plait each other's hair before heading into battle against the Islamic State'.[35]

As an artist committed to truth telling through photo-media, Afshar strategically blurs the lines between documentary and staged images to create space for the stories of the oppressed. For the Iranian born artist, this particular body of work hits closer to home. Despite facing exile for her critique of the Iranian regime, Afshar unapologetically speaks about the series which was 'made in response to the feminist uprising that began in Iran in September 2022, following the death of 22-year-old Jina Amini who had been arrested by Iran's morality police for not wearing the hijab properly'.[36] Afshar centres female power and autonomy through the imagery of women braiding one another's hair stating, 'the twines of a plait are referred to as *pichesh-e-moo* in Farsi, meaning the turn or fold of the hair. A revolution is a turning point, but it is never without loss'.[37]

***

Love is broadly seen as an intimate emotional and/or physical convergence between people. There is also parental and familial love, the love shared between friends, siblings or community. Or there is the ecstasy of finding spiritual or other-worldly love, of annihilation *(fanaa)* and love of the Divine. In this current moment it is not difficult to see love in proximity to the tumult and turmoil of the world. We see love manifesting in great numbers, as solidarity between communities and between complete strangers in various movements across the globe. We also see the love of individuals, and of humanity, and even in nature as a form of resistance, ever evolving, anew. Reflecting upon the words of the great Muslim scholar and poet Jalāl al-Dīn Muḥammad Balkhī, *to love is to risk everything.*[38]

1. Jalāl al-Dīn Muḥammad Balkhī (Rūmī), *Mathnawi* VI 1967-74, translated by Kabir Helminski.
2. See Safdar Ahmad's catalogue essay for this publication for more information on fanaa.
3. Afzal Iqbal, *The Life and Work of Jalal-ud-Din Rumi* The Other Press, Selangor, 2014, pp. 50–110. Jalāl ad-Dīn Muhammad Balkhī, known in the West as Rumi, was an Islamic scholar, theologian, a *Hafiz* (i.e., a Muslim who memorises the entire *Qur'an* by heart without error) and a respected *Imam* (religious leader) who was learned in *Shari'ah* (Islamic jurisprudence). He was born Balkh, in the Greater Iran region (which is known today as Afghanistan). Fearing the brutal Mongolian invasion, Rumi's family migrated to Konya in Türkiye where he famously met his 'spiritual teacher' *Shams of Tabriz*. He spent the remainder of his life teaching the Qur'an, writing poetry, and preaching a mystical form of Islam. After he passed away on 17 December in 1273, his followers created the Mevlevi Sufi Order in his honour.
4. Rumi, *Fragments / Ecstasies*, trans. Daniel Liebert, in Hossein Valamanesh, *The lover circles his own heart*, Museum of Contemporary Art, https://www.mca.com.au/collection/artworks/2005.4A-C/, accessed May 27, 2025. Note: As part of the installation, Valamanesh includes an edited version of the Rumi poem *The lover circles his own heart*. The English translation of the complete verses of the poem from Farsi are as follows: 'We came whirling; Out of nothingness; Scattering stars; Like dust; The stars made a circle; And in the middle' We dance; The wheel of heaven; Circle God; like a mill; If you grab a spoke; It will tear your hand off; Turning and turning; It sunders; All attachment; Were that wheel not in love; it would cry; Enough! How long this turning?; Every atom; Turns bewildered; Beggars circle table; Dogs circle carrion; The lover circles his own heart; Ashamed; I circle shame; A ruined water wheel; Whichever way I turn; Is the river; If that rusty old sky; Creaks to a stop; Still, still I turn; And it is God only; circling Himself'.
5. Hossein Valamanesh, *The lover circles his own heart*, Museum of Contemporary Art, https://www.mca.com.au/collection/artworks/2005.4A-C/, accessed May 27, 2025.
6. The Threshold Society, 'Sema: The Universal Movement', https://sufism.org/sema-3/sema/sema-the-universal-movement-by-dr-celaleddin-b-celebi-2, accessed May 27, 2025. The Threshold Society provides a detailed account of the practice of 'Whirling Dervishes', known as *sema* (the person performing *sema* is called a *semazen*), stating: 'Contrary to popular belief, the *semazen's* goal is not to lose consciousness or to fall into a state of ecstasy. Instead, by revolving in harmony with all things in nature—with the smallest cells and with the stars in the firmament—the *semazen* testifies to the existence and the majesty of the Creator, thinks of Him, gives thanks to Him, and prays to Him. In so doing, the *semazen* confirms the words of the Qur'an (64:1): *Whatever is in the skies or on earth invokes God.* An important characteristic of this seven-centuries-old ritual is that it unites the three fundamental components of human nature: the mind (as knowledge and thought), the heart (through the expression of feelings, poetry, and music) and the body (by activating life, by the turning). These three elements are thoroughly joined both in theory and in practice as perhaps in no other ritual or system of thought. The *Sema* ceremony represents the human being's spiritual journey, an ascent by means of intelligence and love to Perfection (*Kemal*). Turning toward the truth, he grows through love, transcends the ego, meets the truth, and arrives at Perfection. Then he returns from this spiritual journey as

one who has reached maturity and completion, able to love and serve the whole of creation and all creatures without discriminating in regard to belief, class, or race.

7. Khaled Sabsabi, statement supplied, March 27, 2025.
8. Ibid.
9. Sahih Muslim, Riyad as-Salihin 1846, Book 18: 'The Book of Miscellaneous Ahadith of Significant Values', Chapter 370: 'Ahadith about Dajjal and Portents of the Hour.' According to Hadith (Islamic Prophetic tradition) *''Aishah (May Allah be pleased with her) reported: The Messenger of Allah (PBUH) said, "Angels were created from light, jinns were created from a smokeless flame of fire, and 'Adam was created from that which you have been told (i.e., sounding clay like the clayof pottery).'* [Sahih Muslim]
10. Khaled Sabsabi, statement supplied, March 27, 2025.
11. Ali Tahayori, statement supplied, March 27, 2025.
12. Ibid.
13. Ali Tahayori, *Archive of longing*, THIS IS NO FANTASY, https://thisisnofantasy.com/exhibition/at-photolondon-24, accessed June 7, 2025.
14. Ali Tahayori, statement supplied, March 27, 2025.
15. Abdul-Rahman Abdullah, statement supplied, March 24, 2025.
16. Ibid.
17. Ibid.
18. Larissa Sansour and Søren Lind, statement supplied, March 21, 2025.
19. Ibid.
20. Ibid.
21. Yhonnie Scarce, statement supplied, April 16, 2025.
22. Ibid.
23. D Harding, statement supplied, March 27, 2025
24. Ibid.
25. 'Megan Cope: The tide waits for no-one,' Queensland Gallery | Gallery of Modern Art, https://www.qagoma.qld.gov.au/stories/megan-cope-creates-artworks-that-are-respectful-to-the-environment/#:~:text=In%20The%20tide%20waits%20for,Traditional%20Owners%2C%20the%20Quandamooka%20people, accessed June 9, 2025.
26. Megan Cope, statement supplied, April 17, 2025.
27. Ibid.
28. Eugenia Flynn, statement supplied, April 17, 2025.
29. Ibid.
30. Ibid.
31. Saodat Ismailova, statement supplied, March 25, 2025.
32. Ibid.
33. Ibid.
34. Hoda Afshar, statement supplied, March 27, 2025.
35. Ibid.
36. Ibid.
37. Ibid.
38. Jalāl al-Dīn Muḥammad Balkhī (Rūmī), *Mathnawi VI* 1967-74, translated by Kabir Helminski.

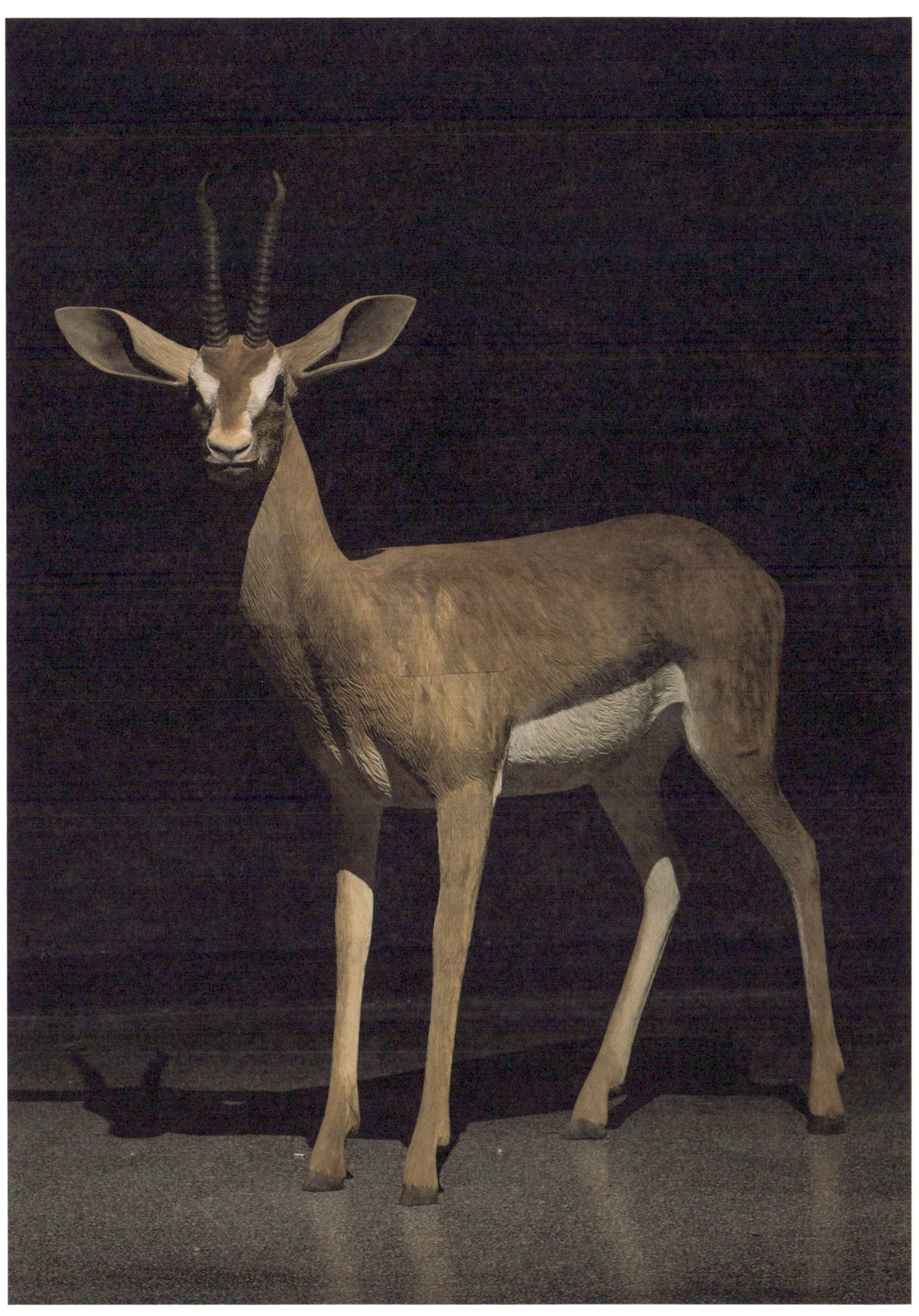

Abdul-Rahman Abdullah, *Witness* 2025, painted wood, horn, glass eyes, 110.0 x 37.0 x 107.0 cm. Acknowledgment: Department of Local Government, Sports & Cultural Industries, WA. Courtesy the artist and Moore Contemporary, Perth

Installation Views

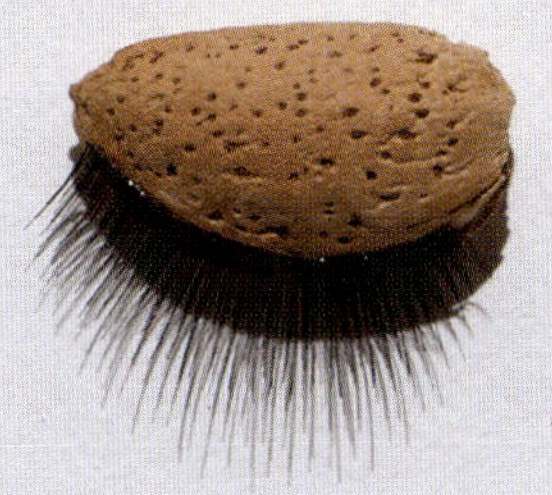
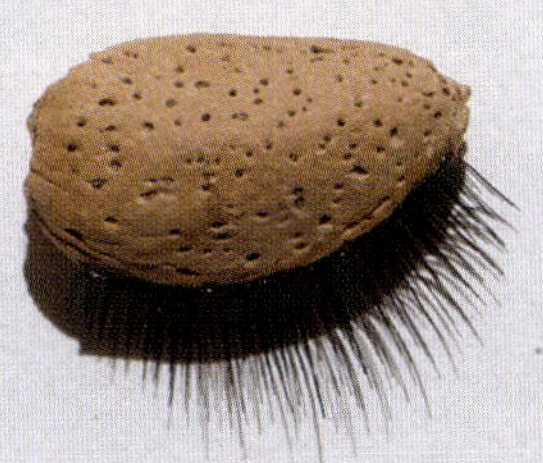

IN PRAISE OF THE BELOVED

H.V. 2006 A/P

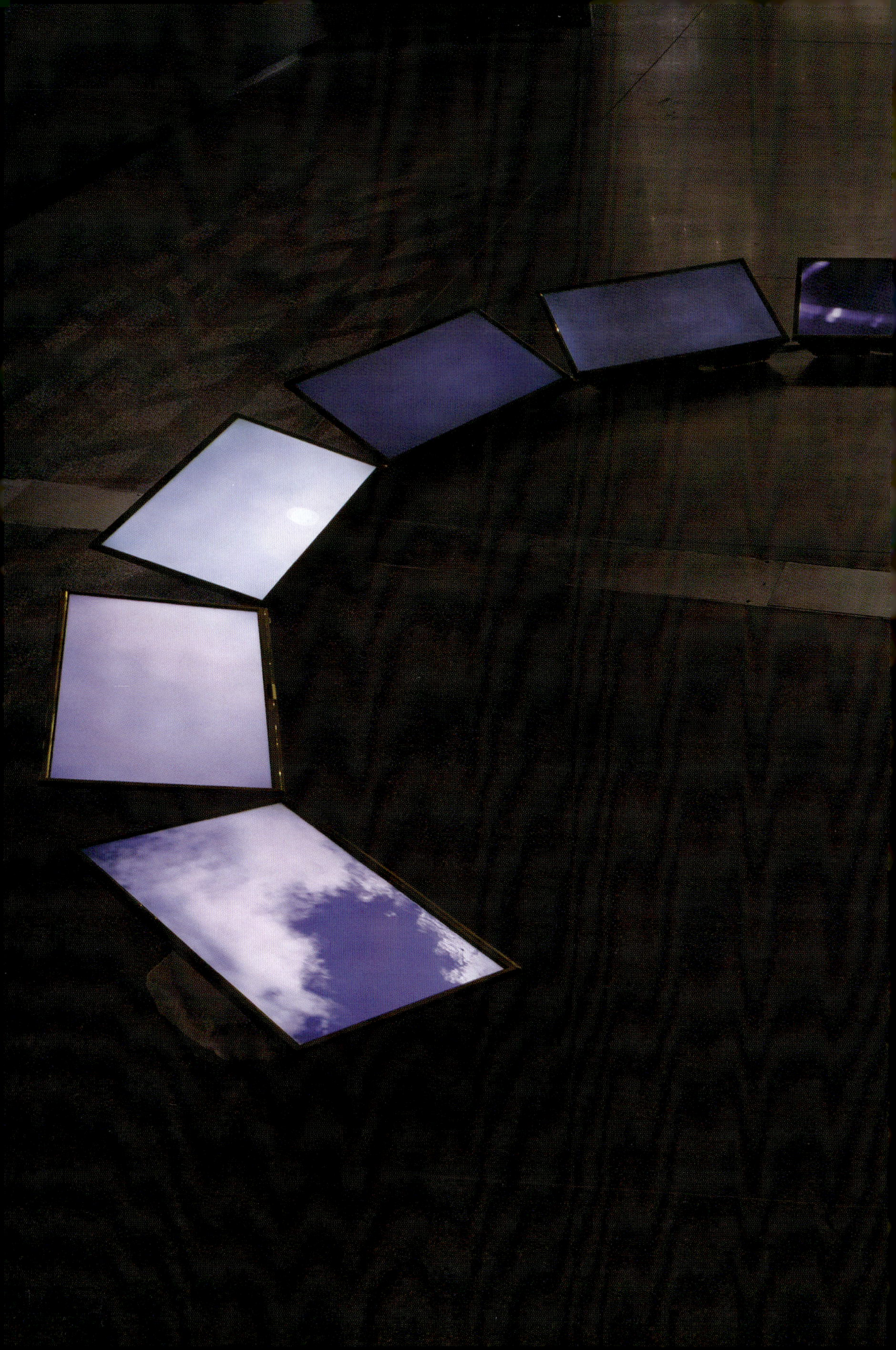

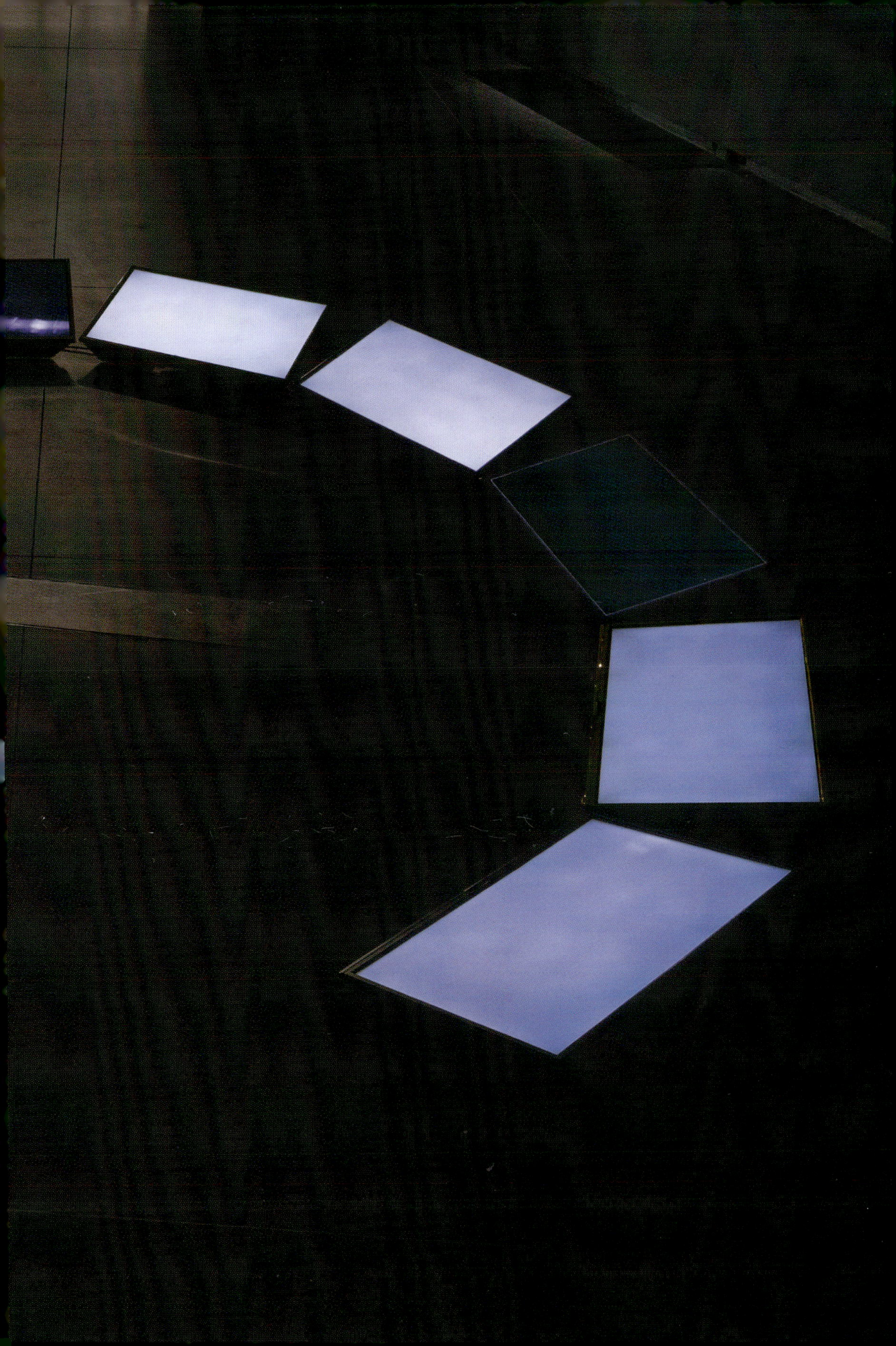

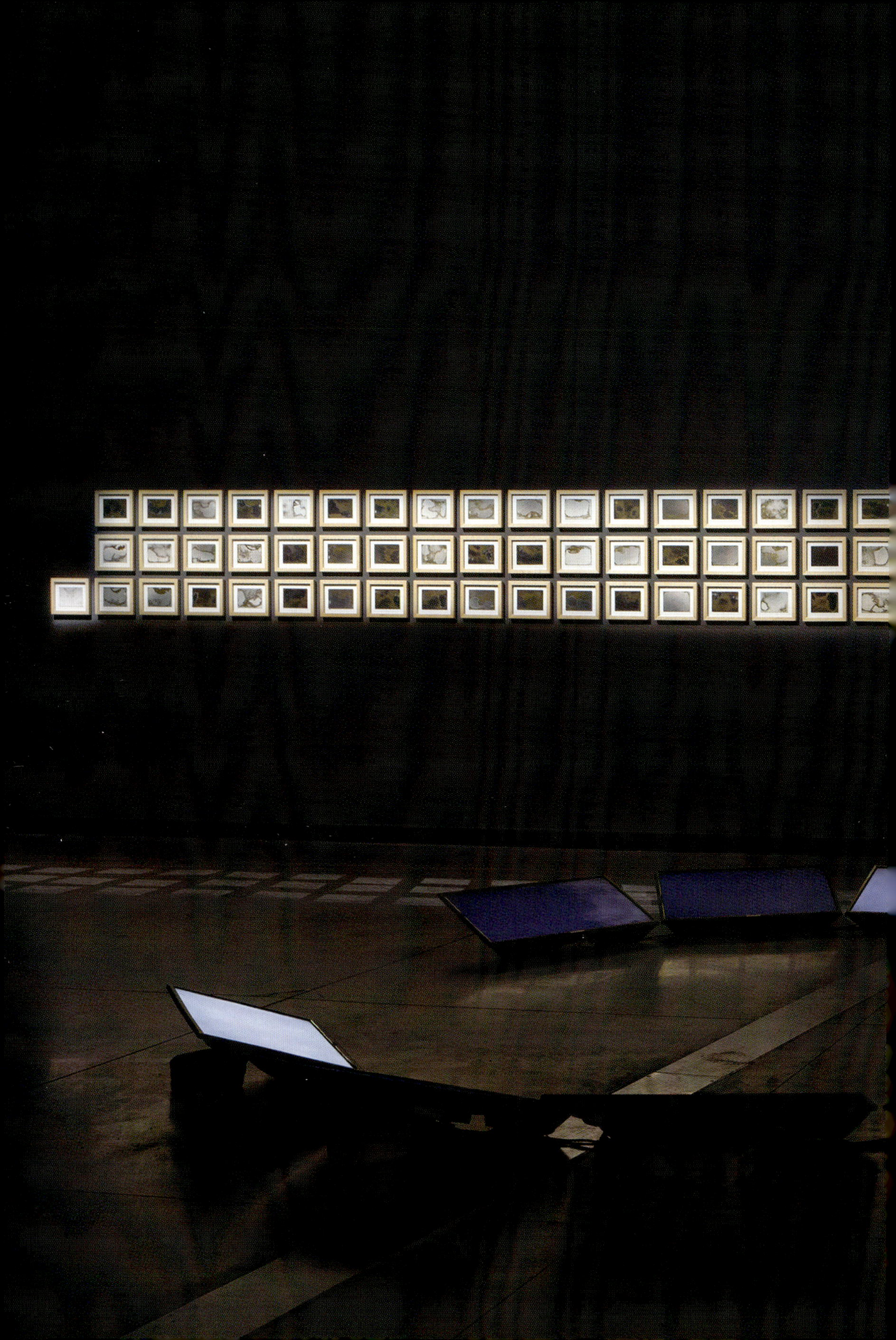

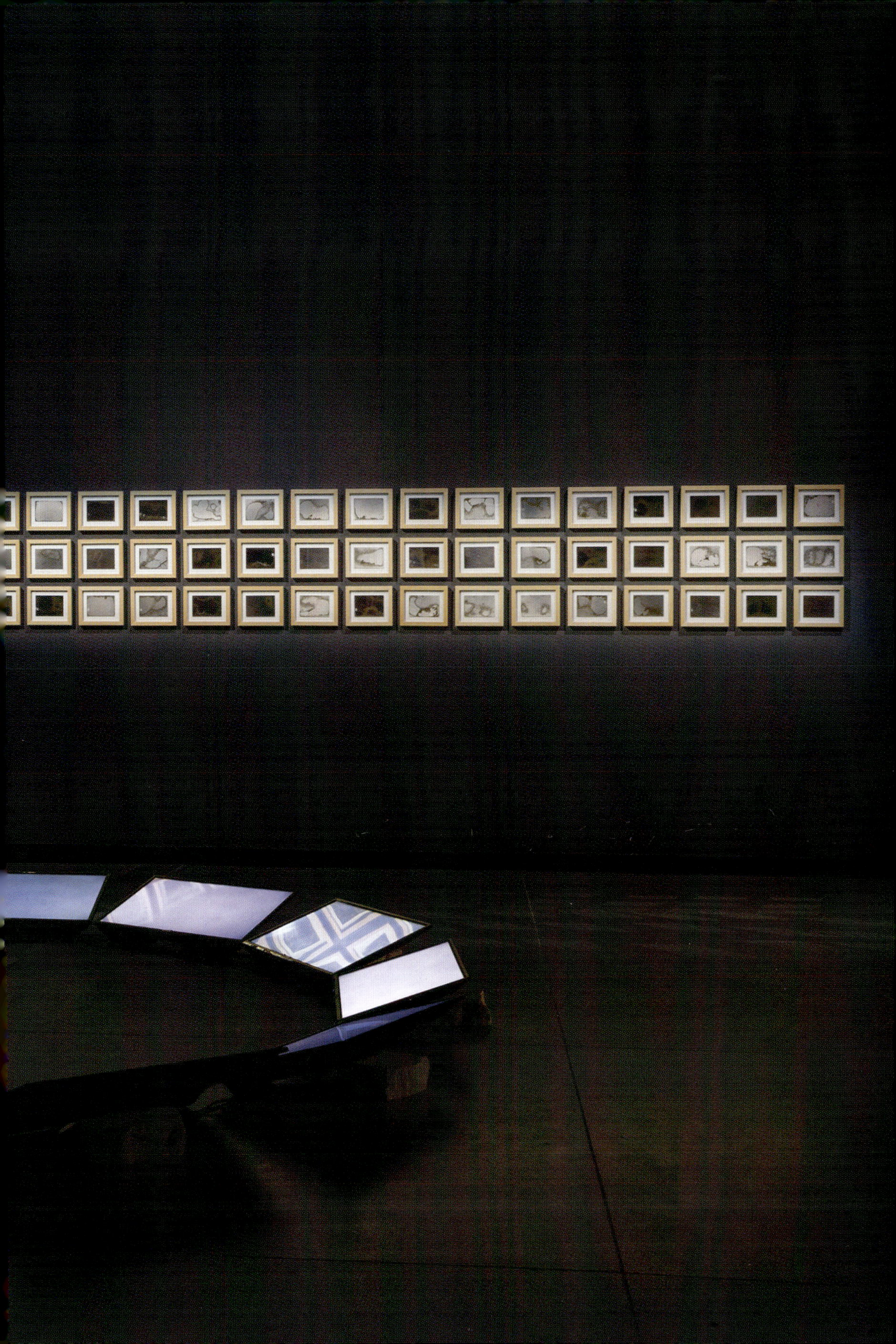

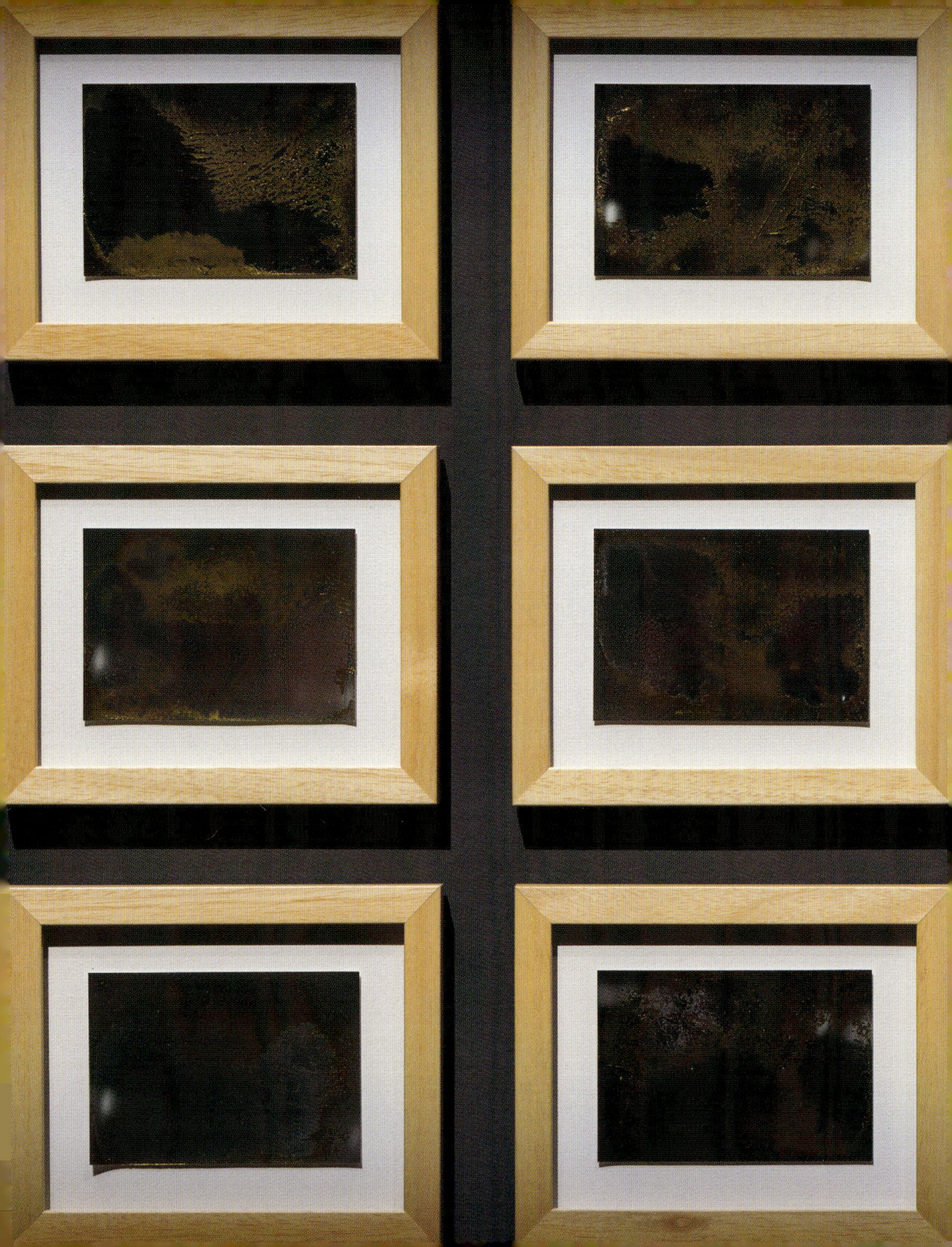

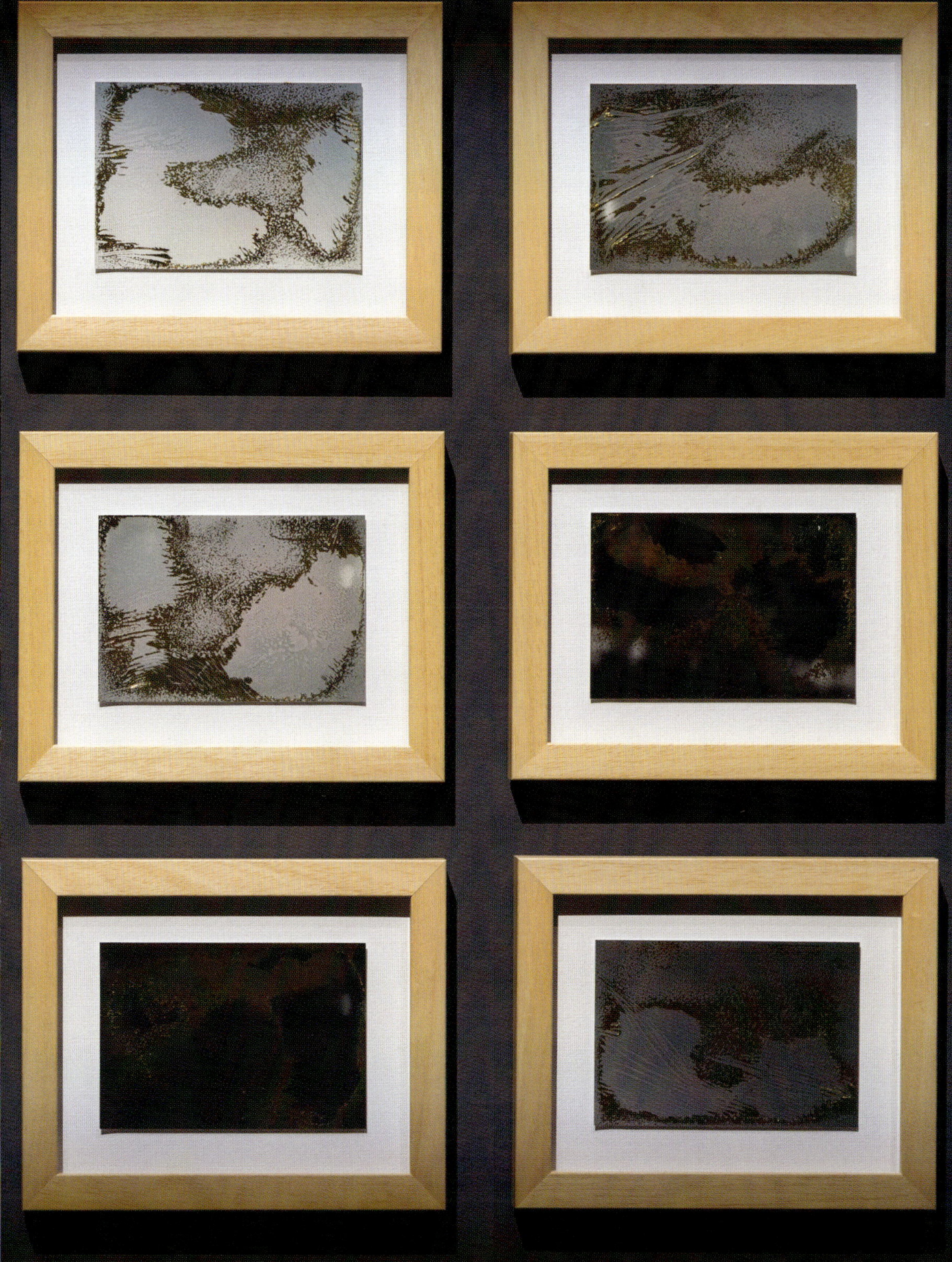

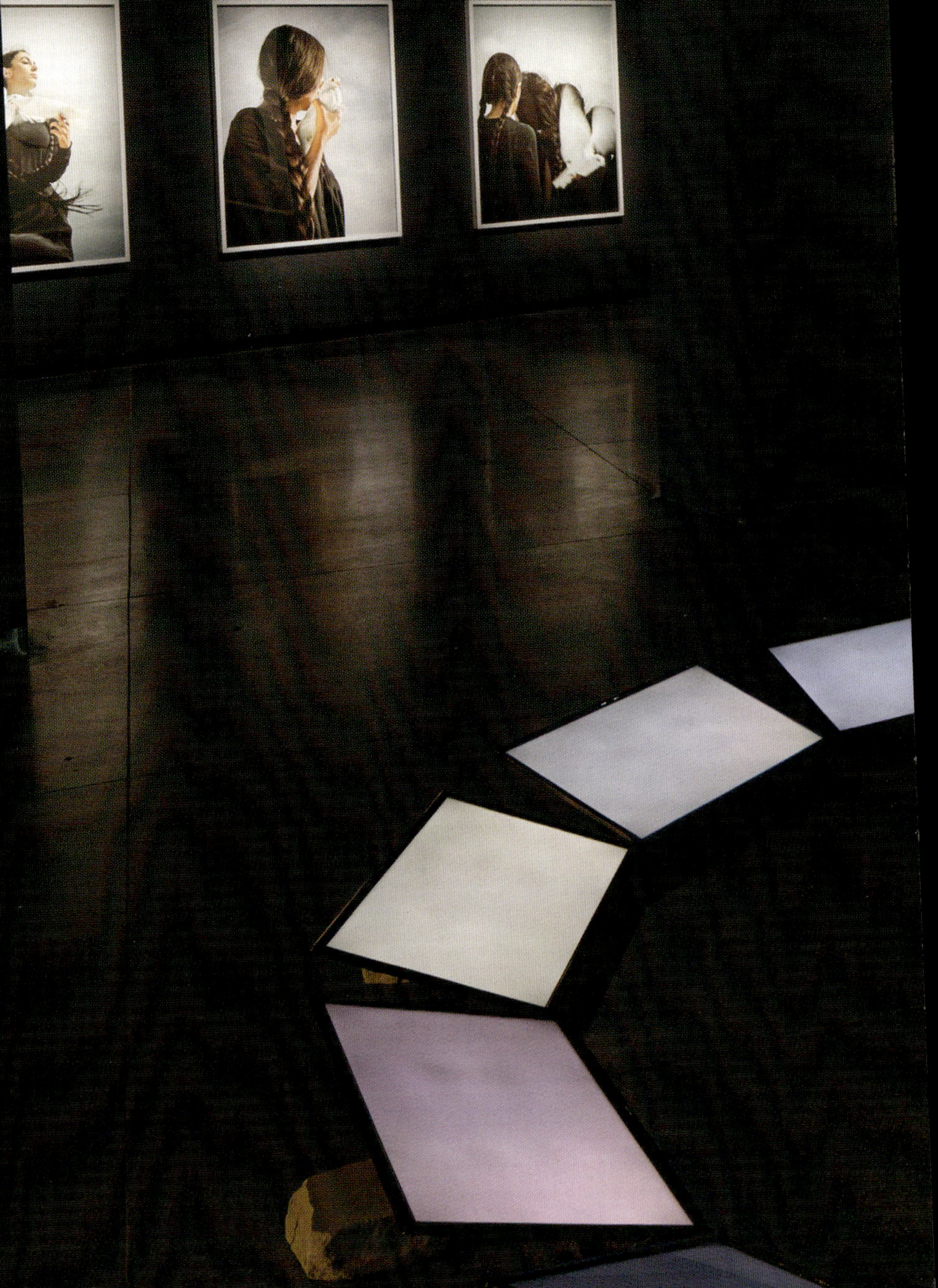

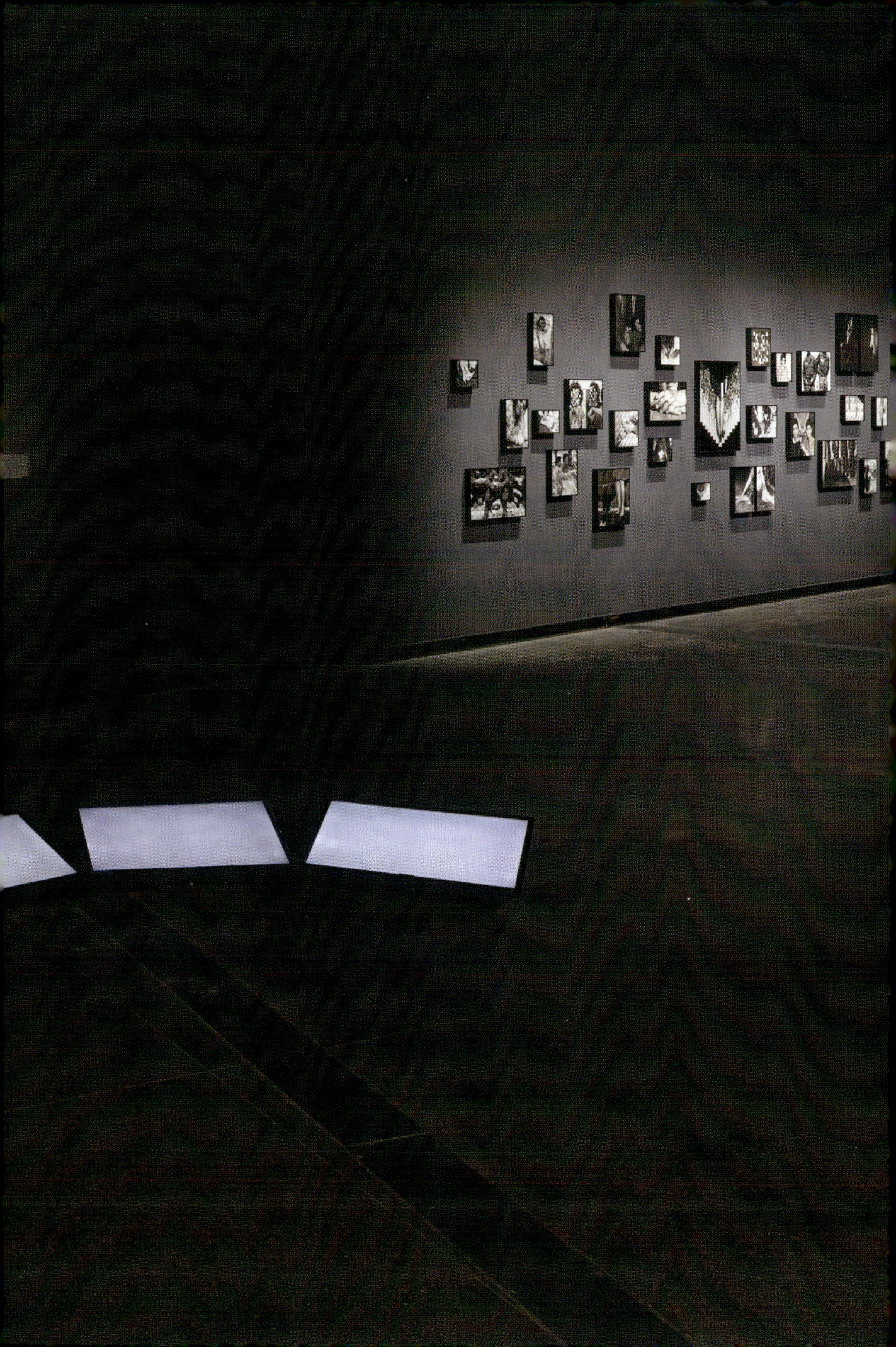

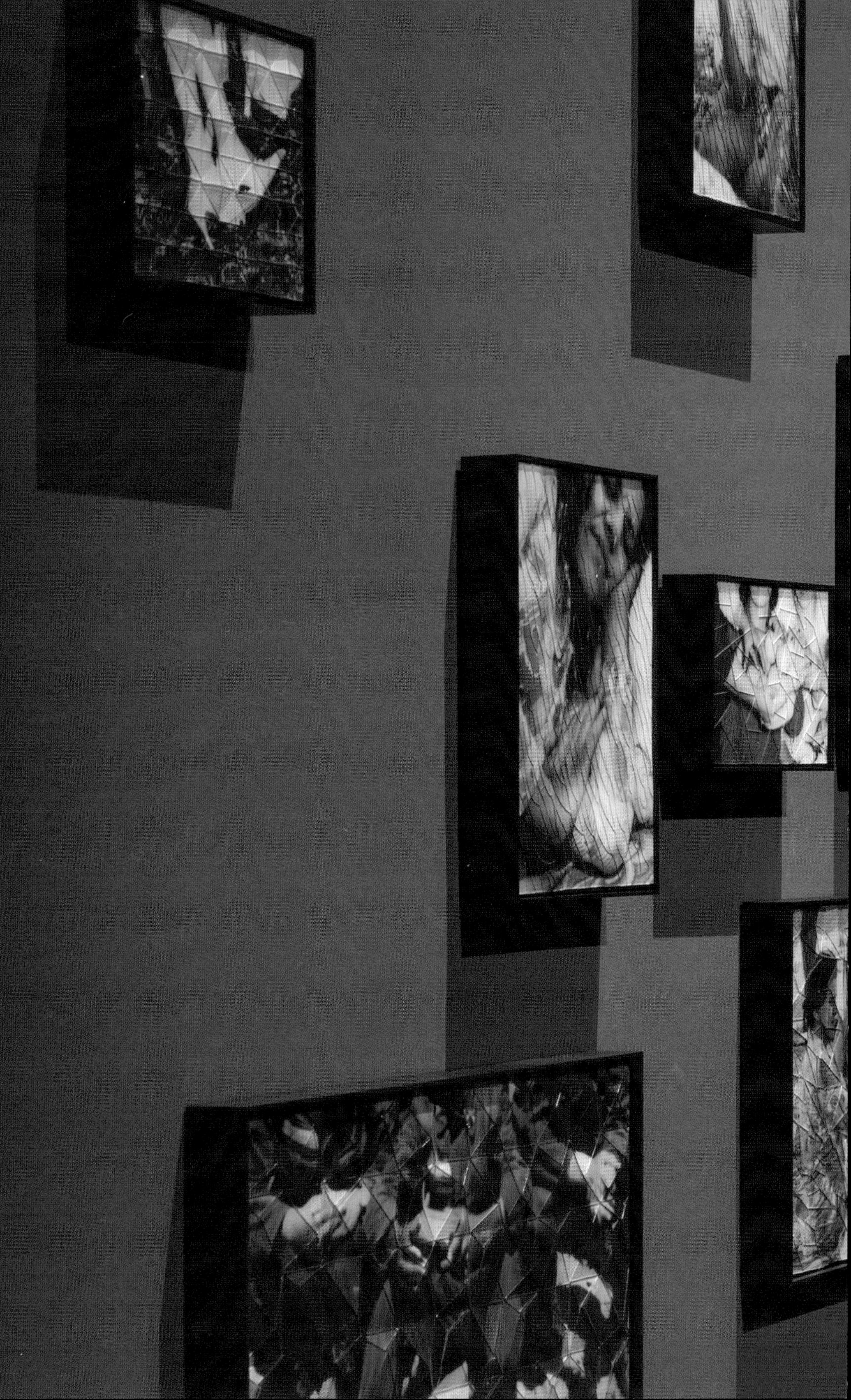

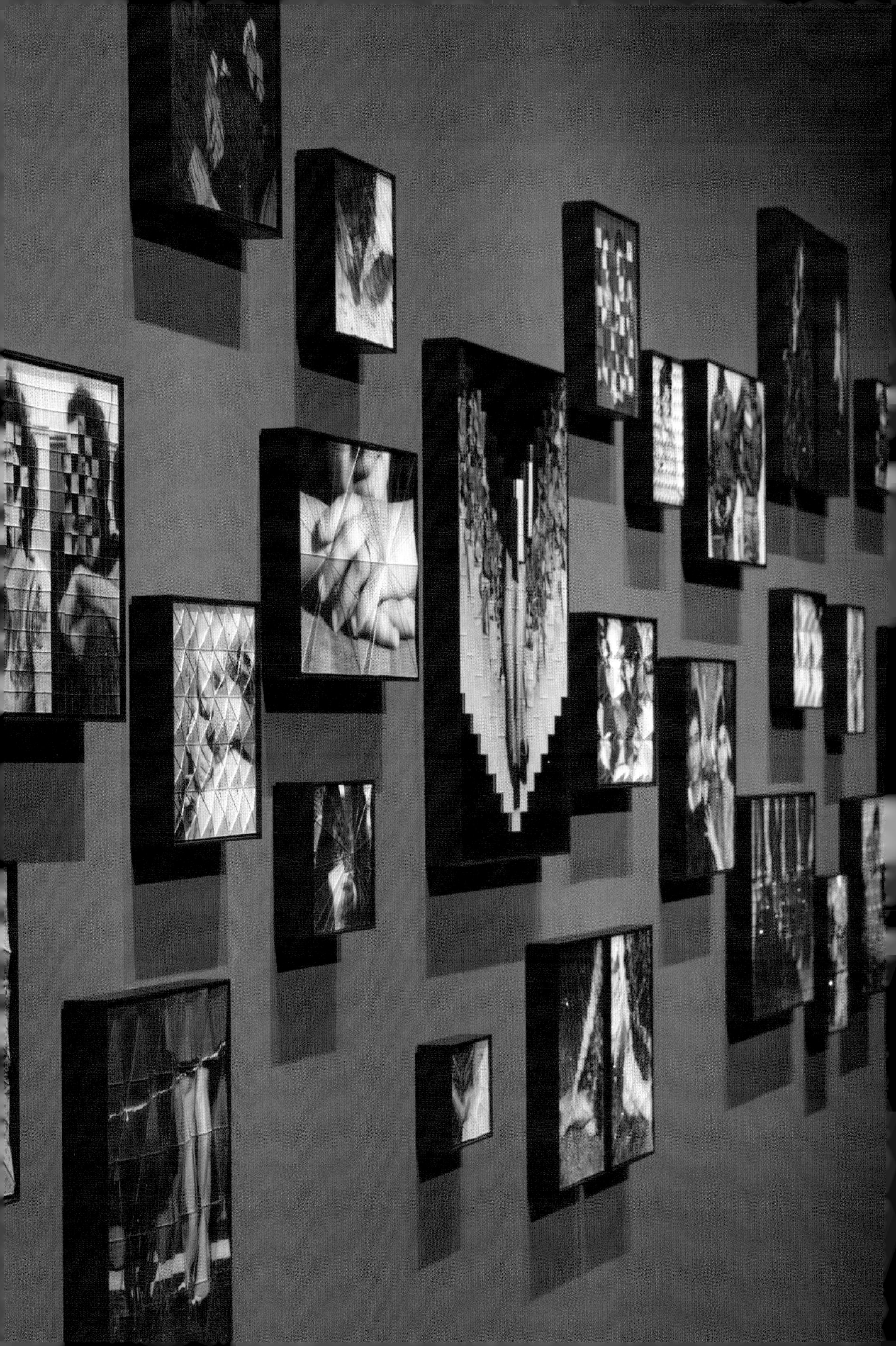

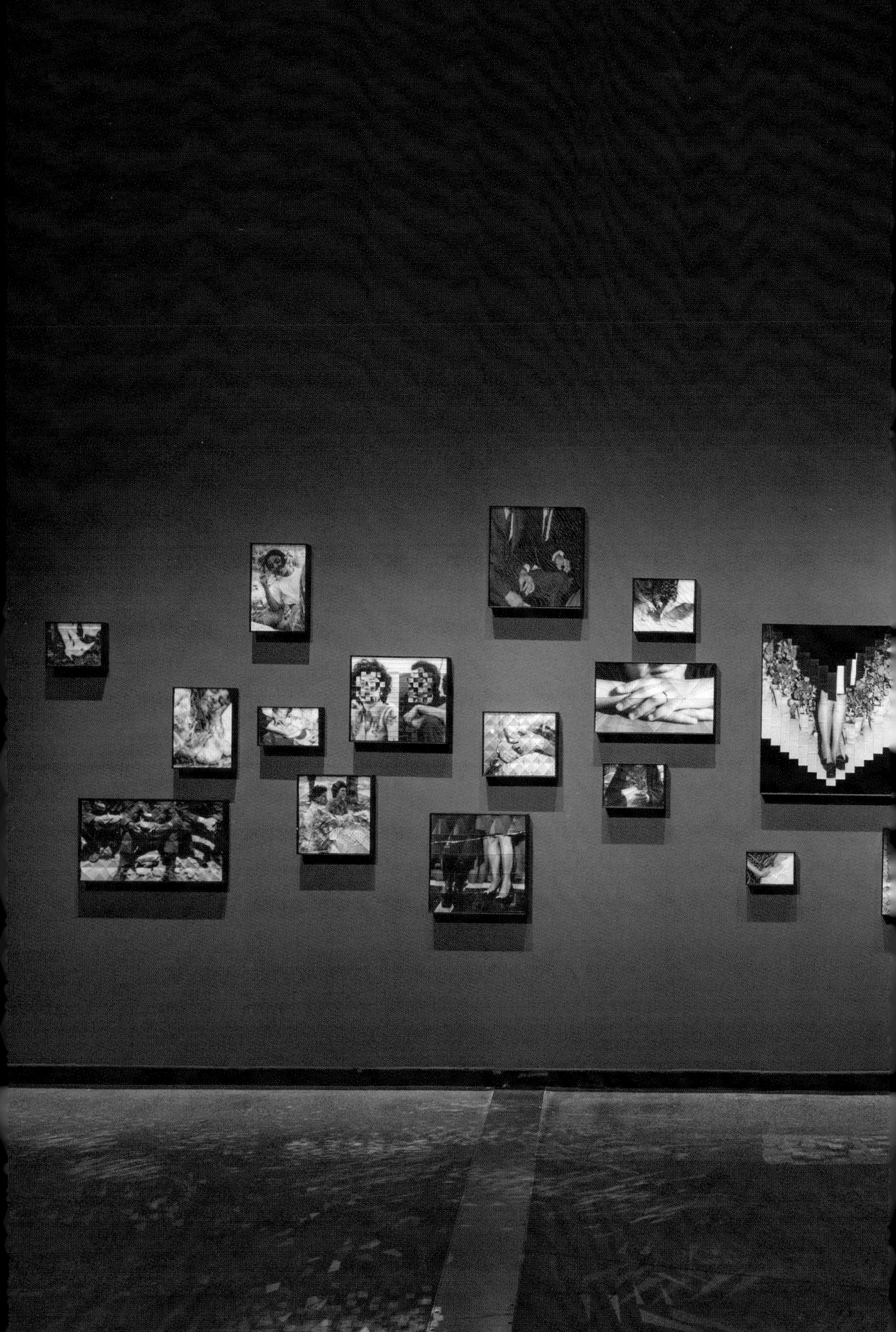

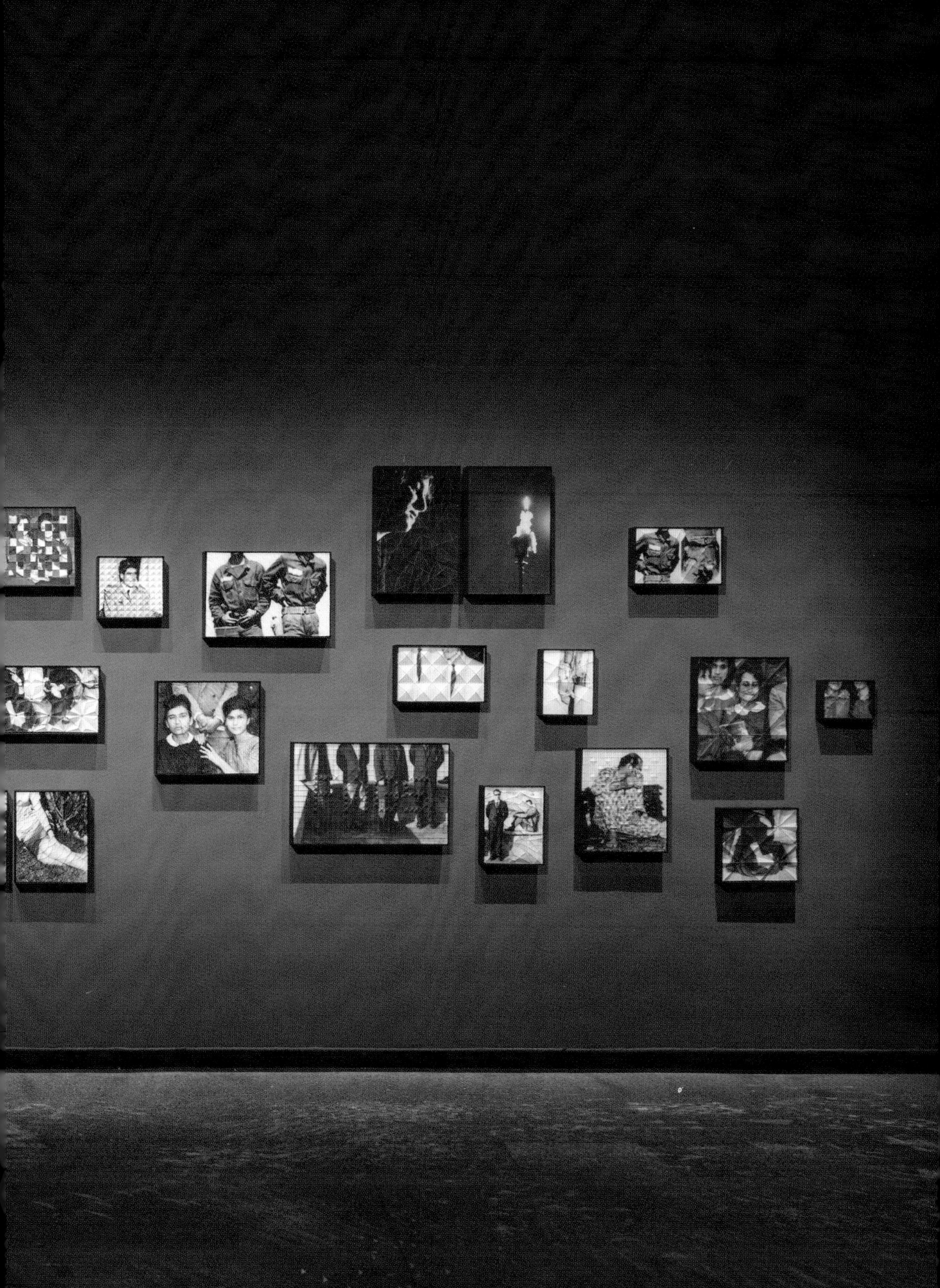

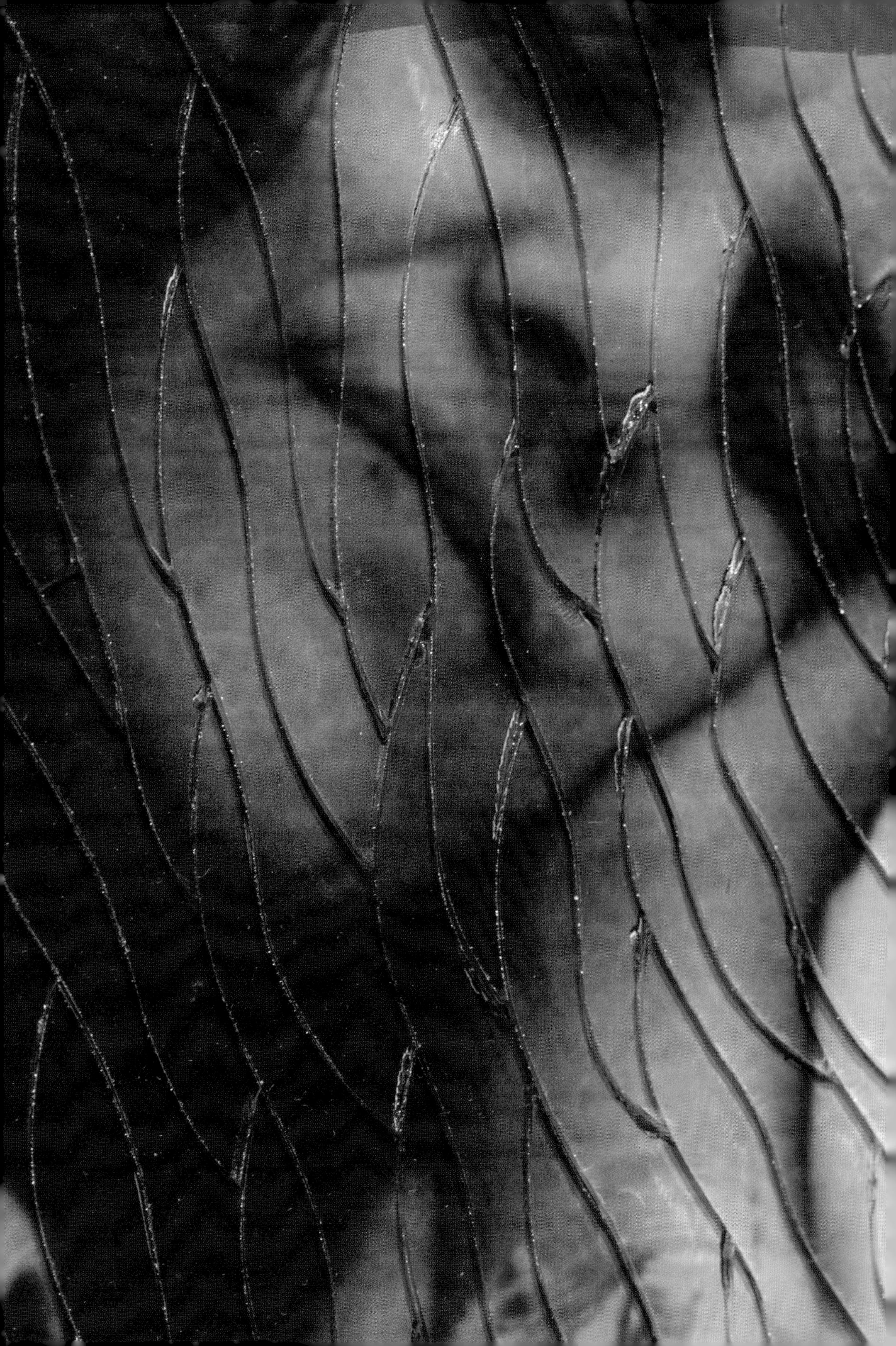

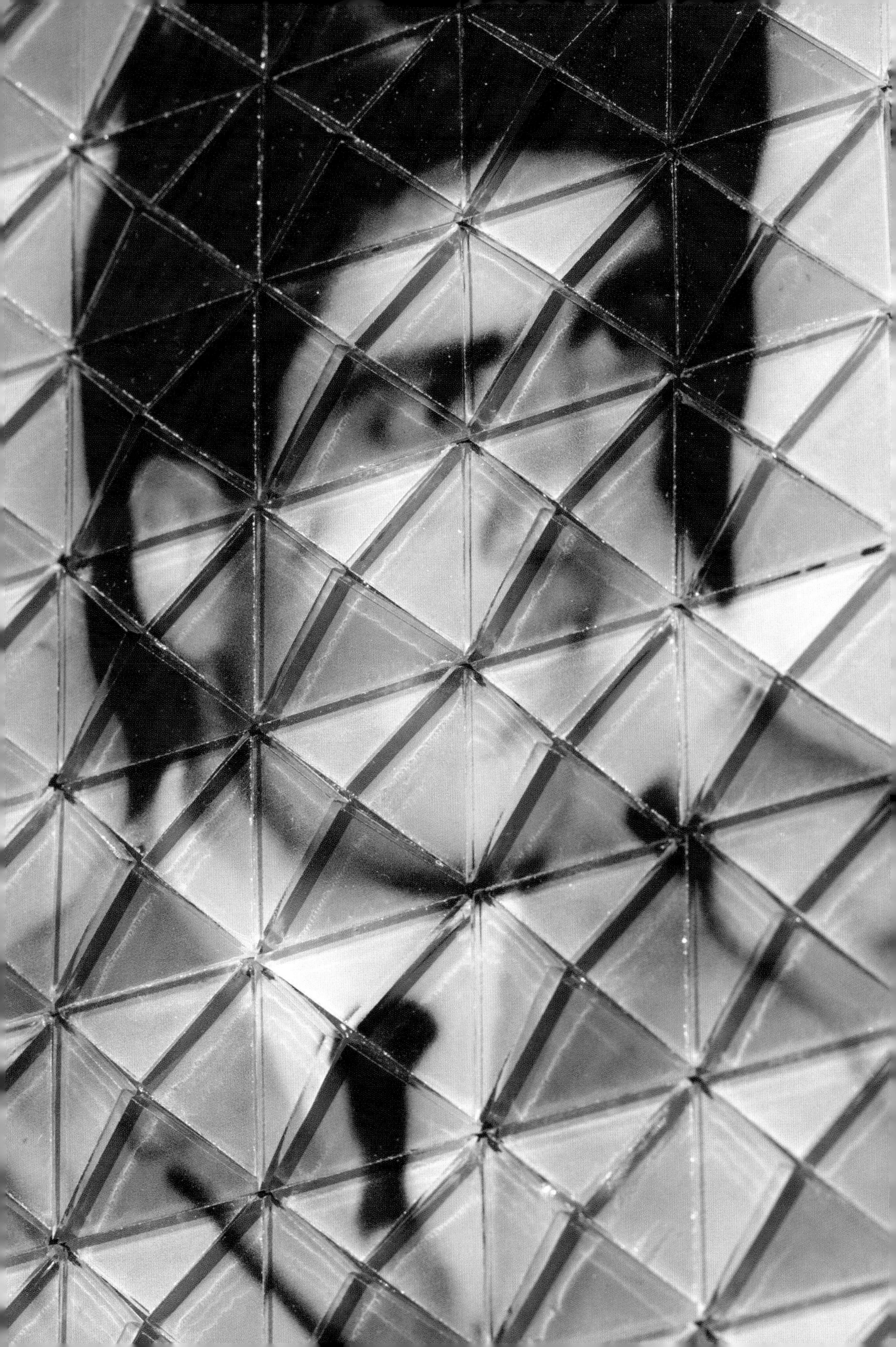

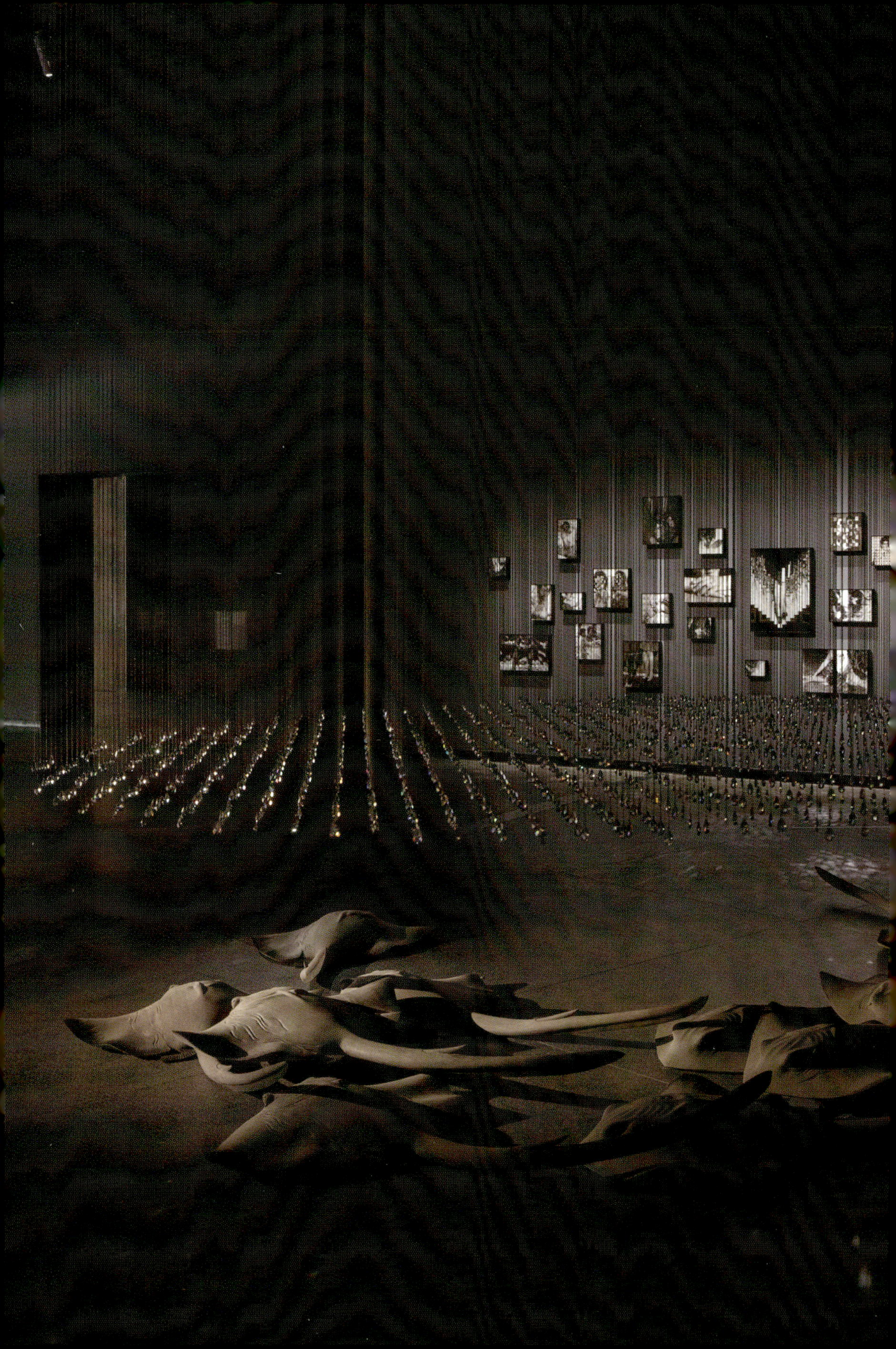

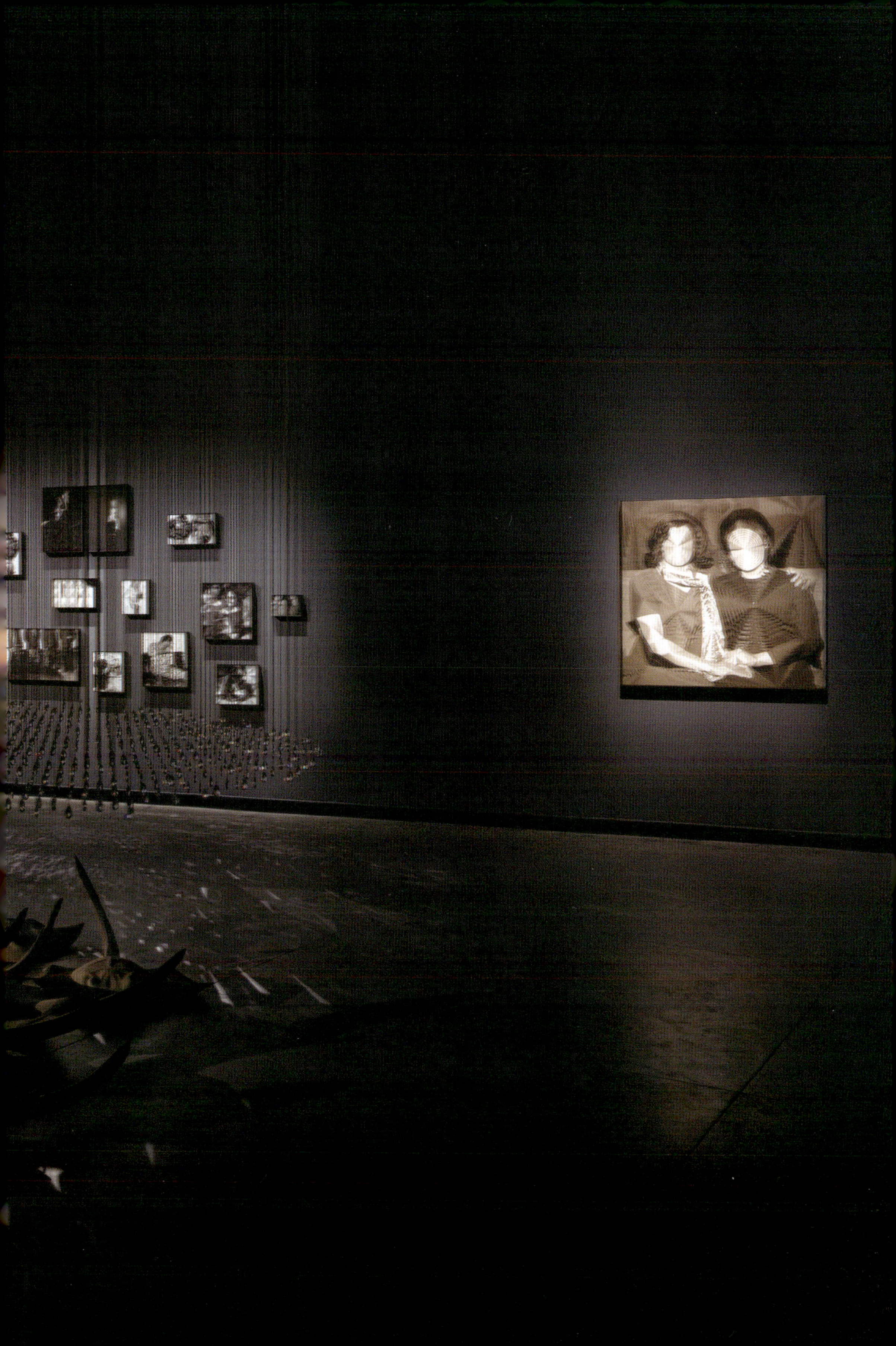

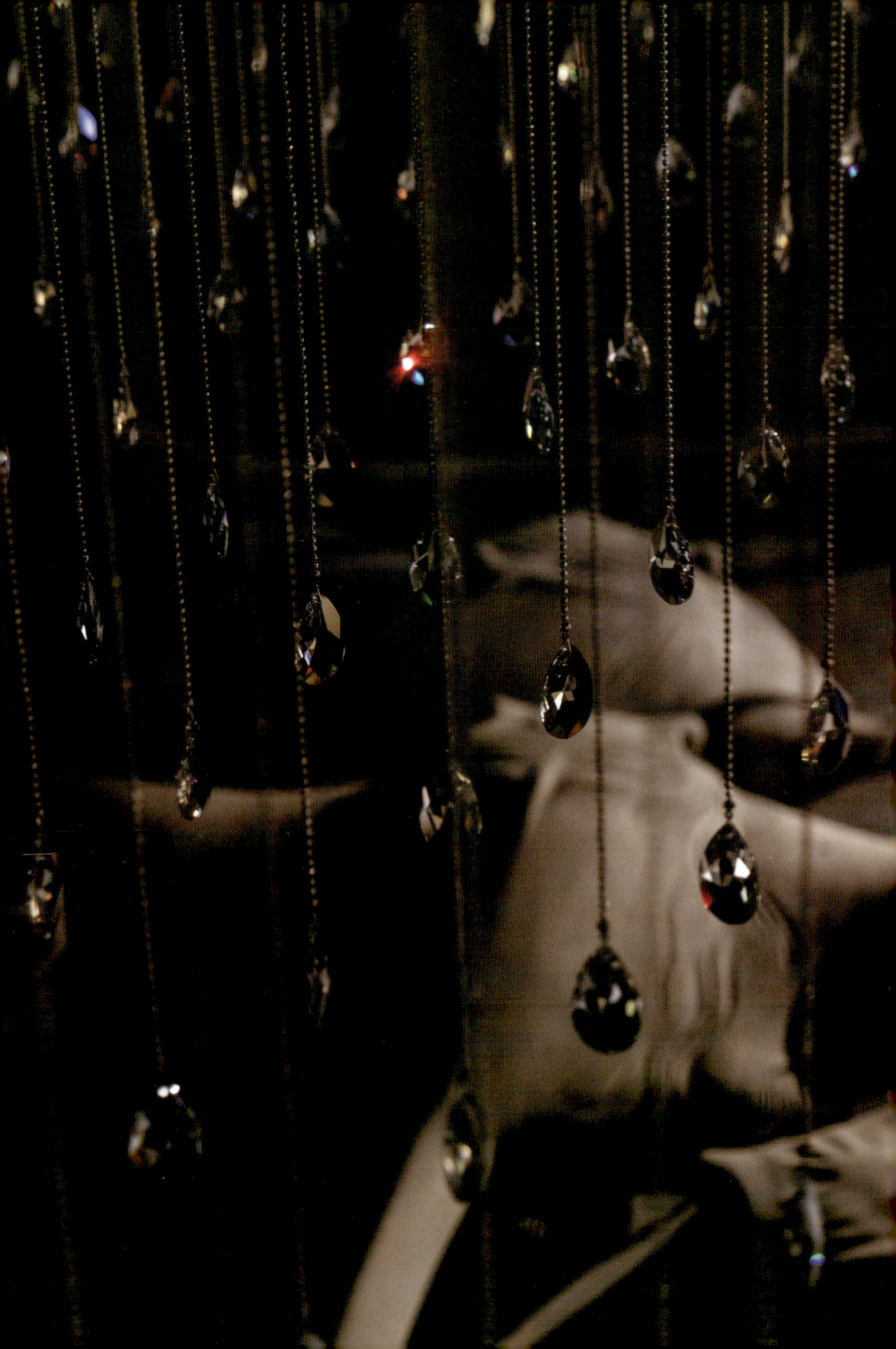

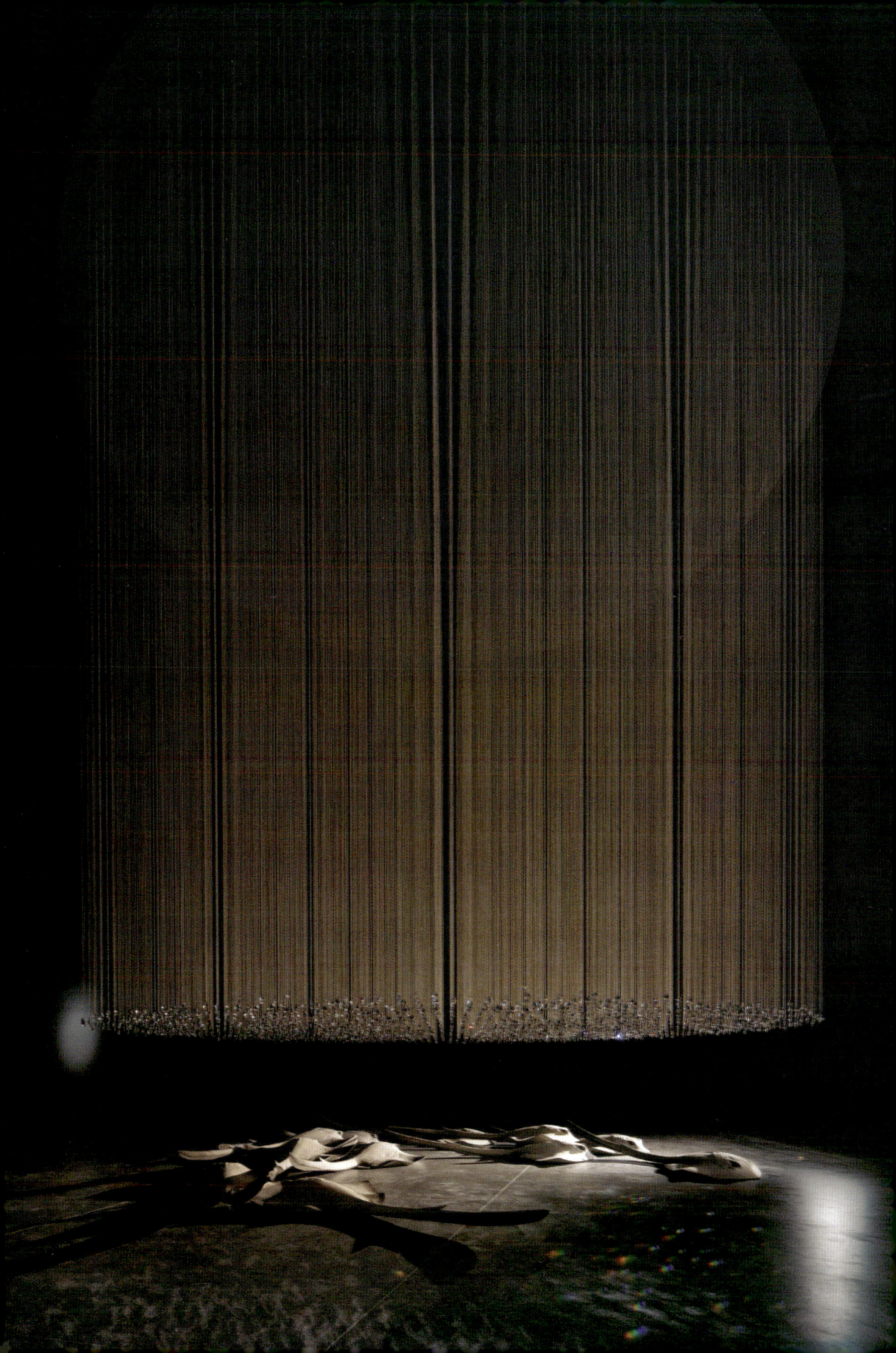

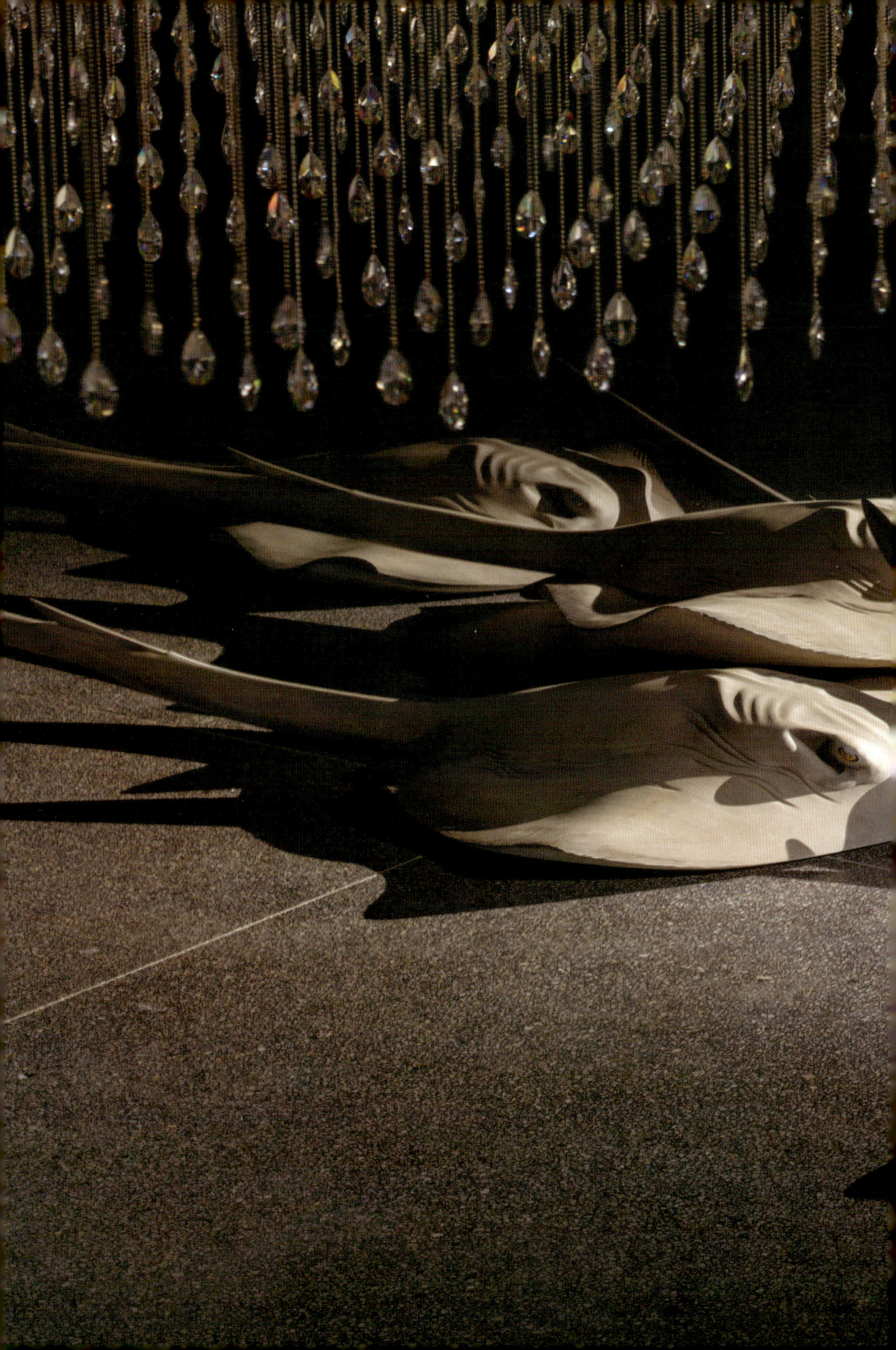

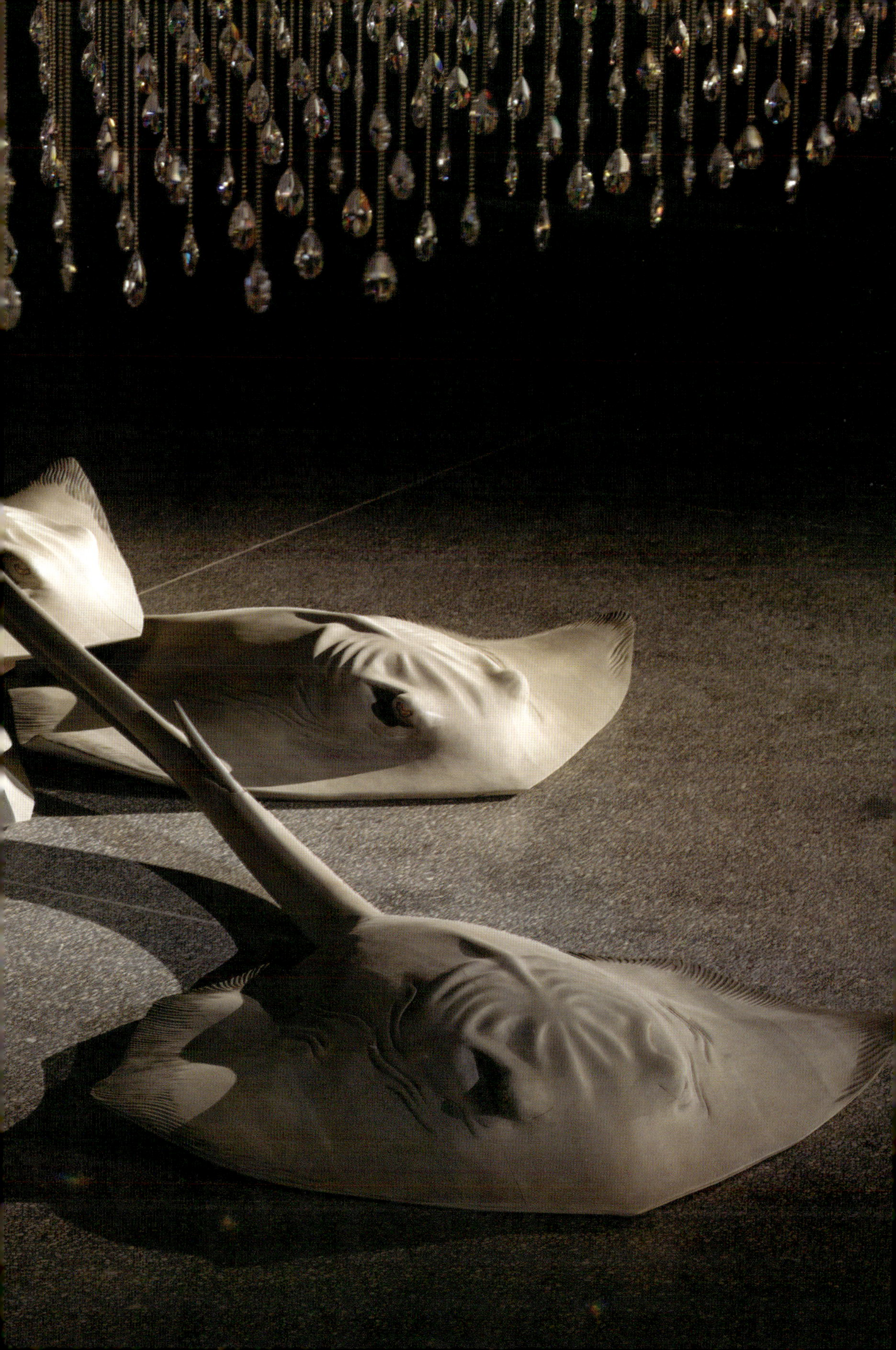

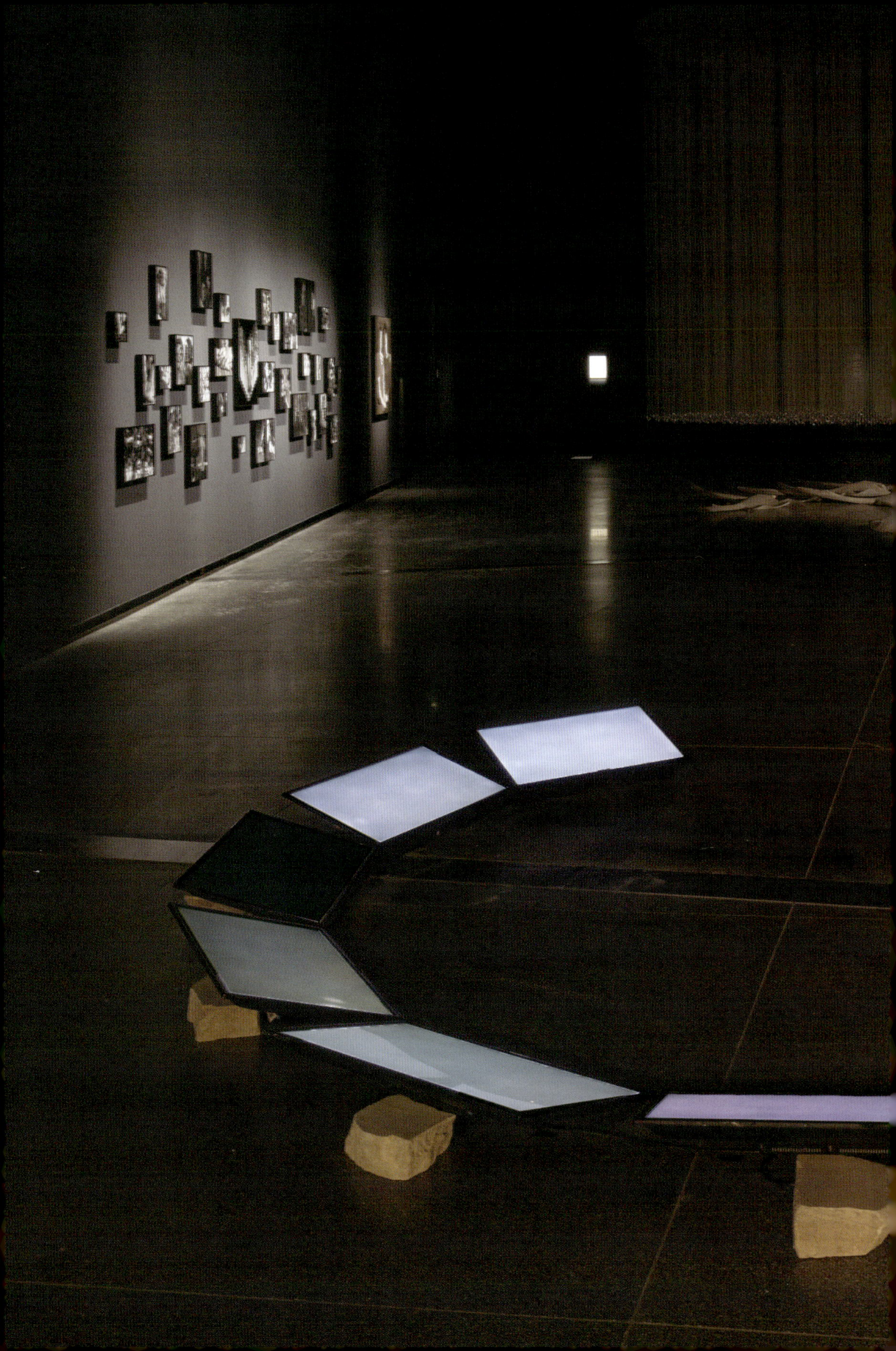

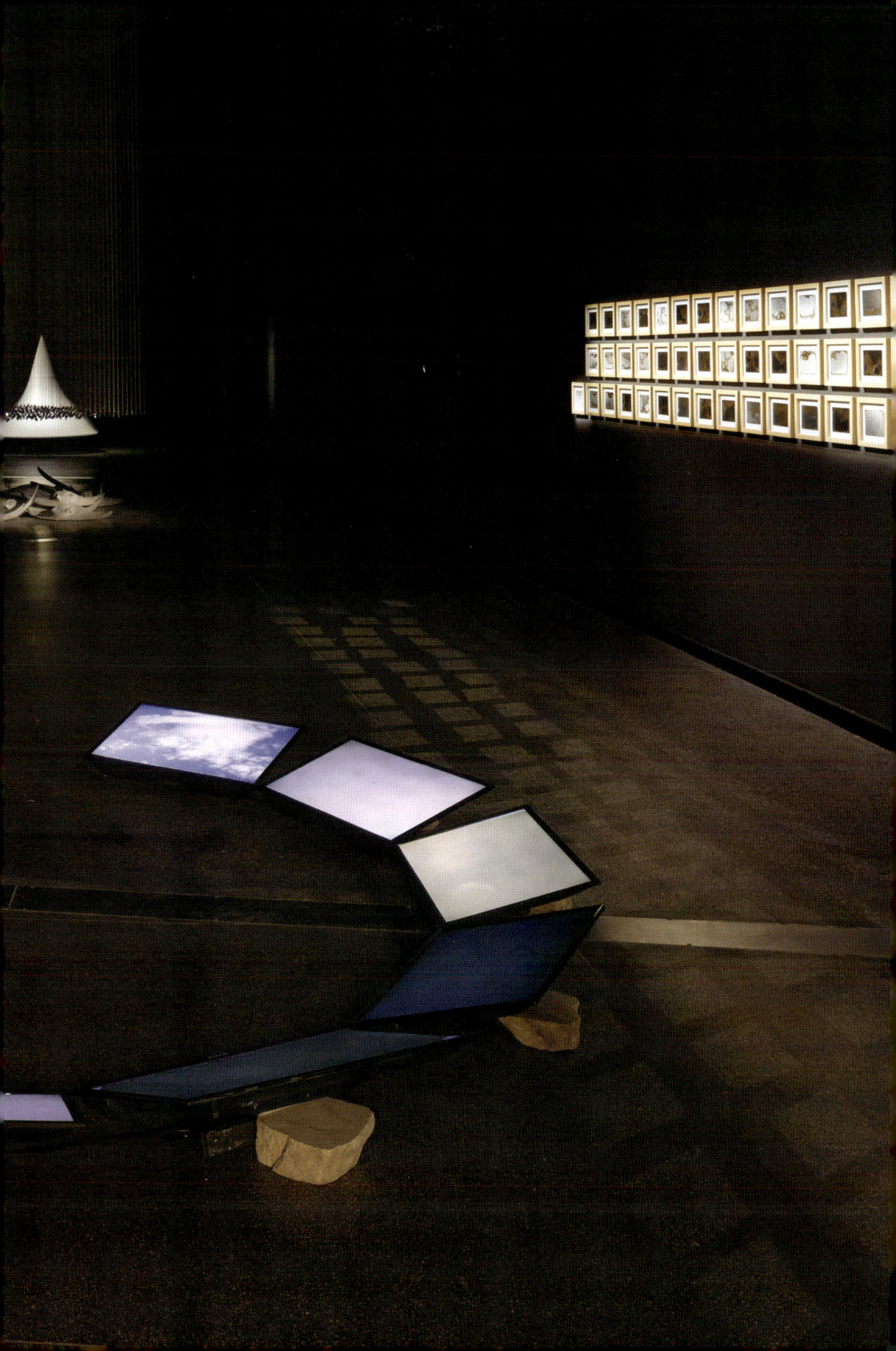

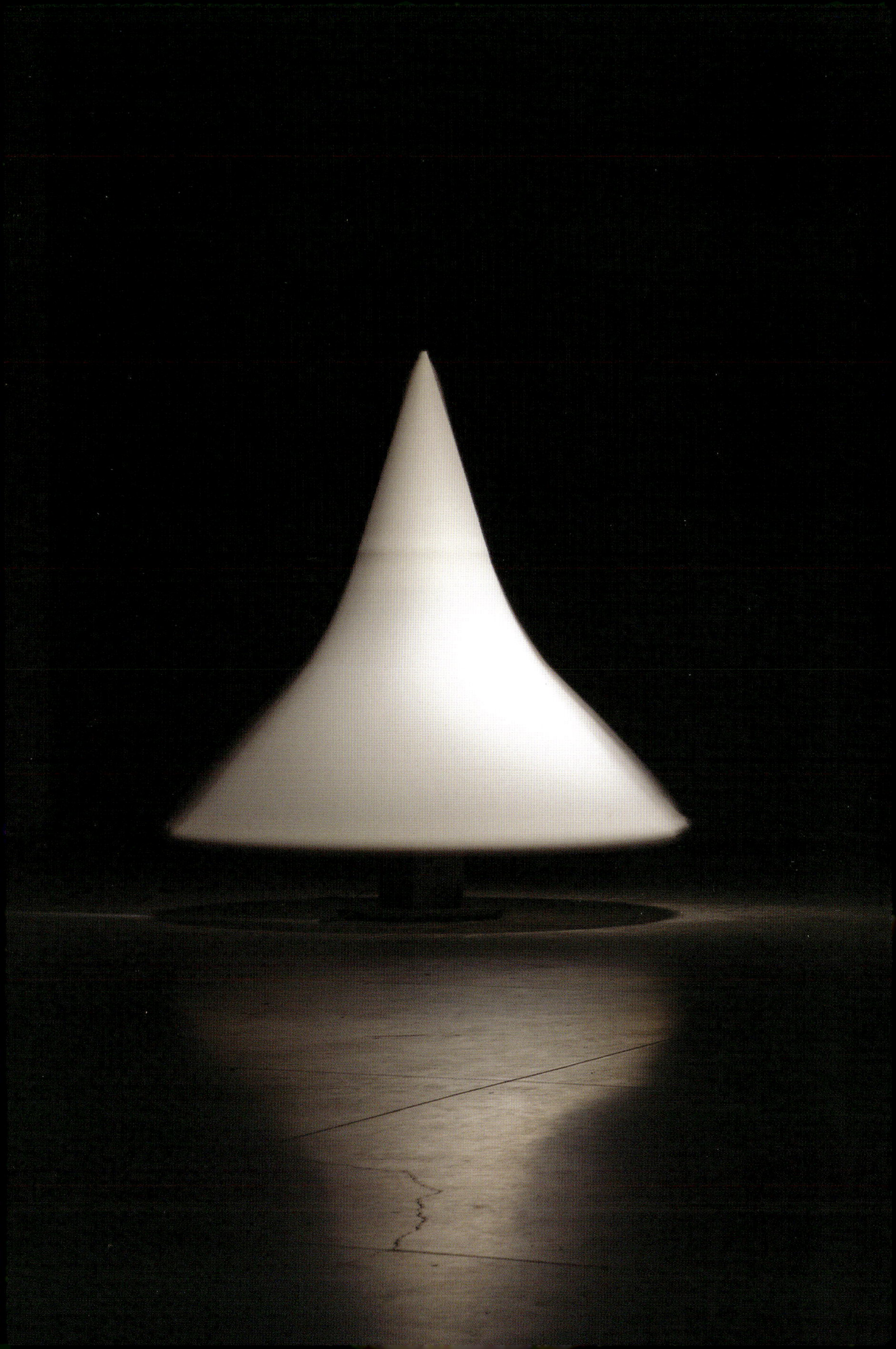

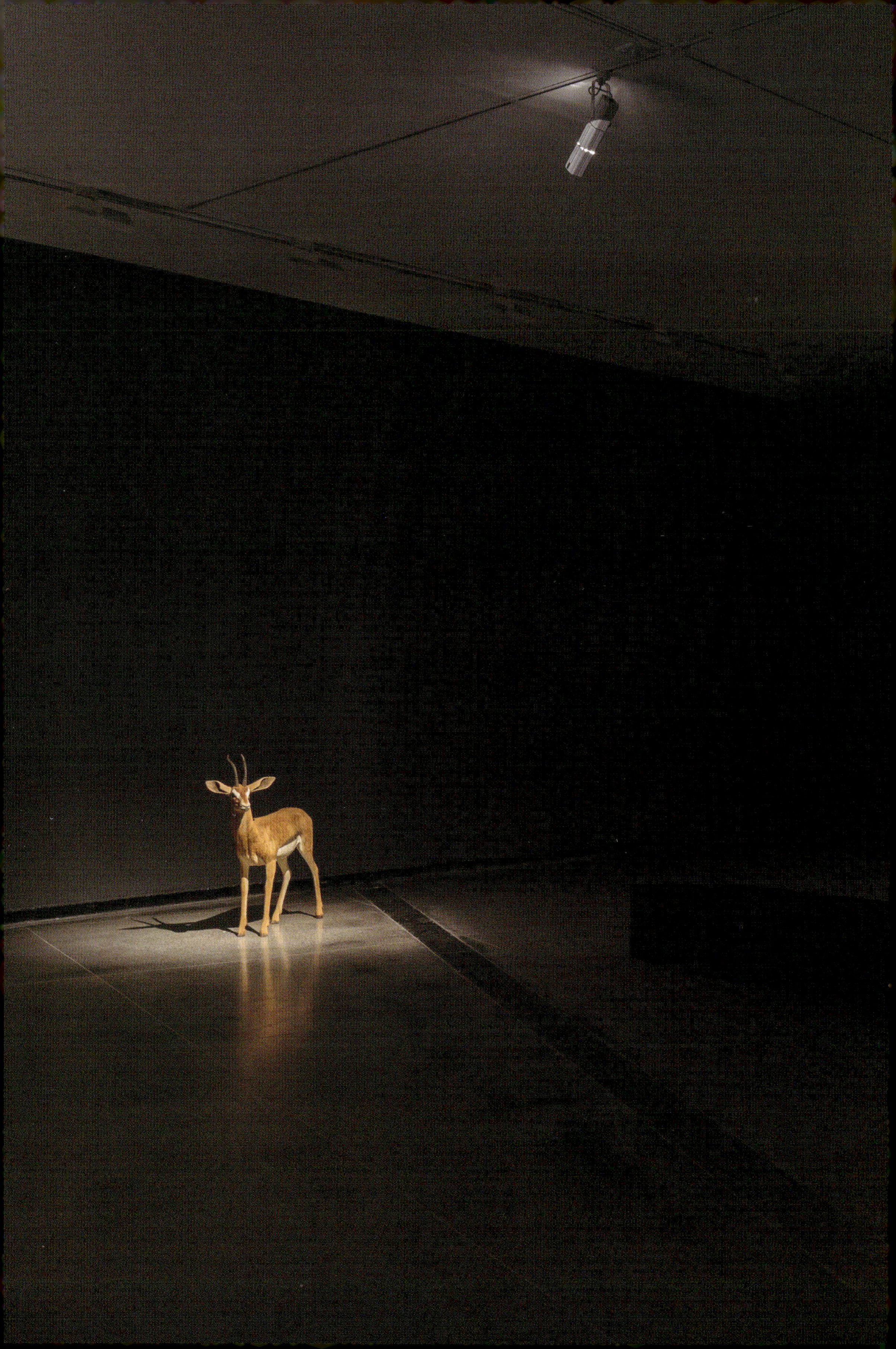

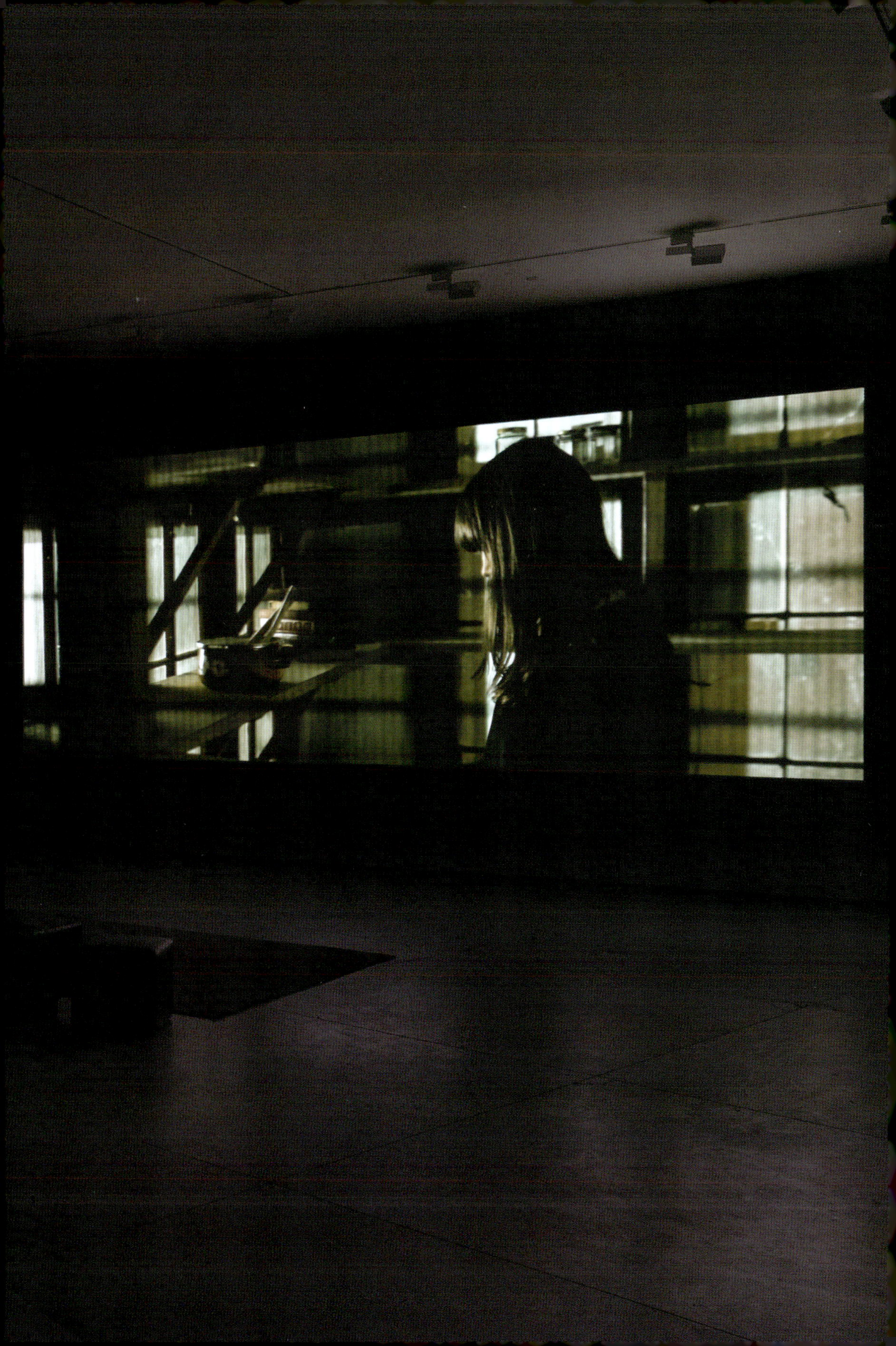

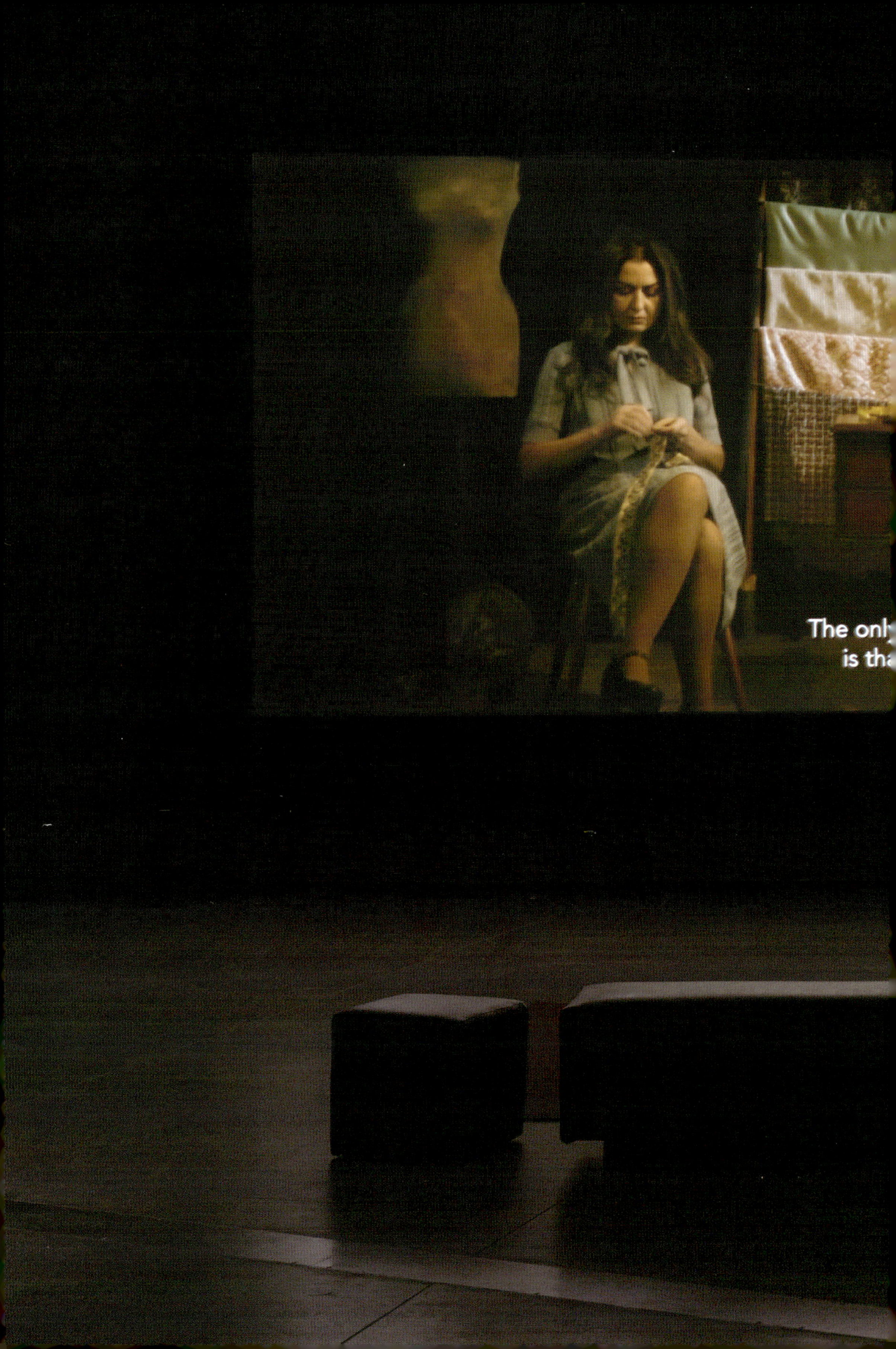
The onl
is tha

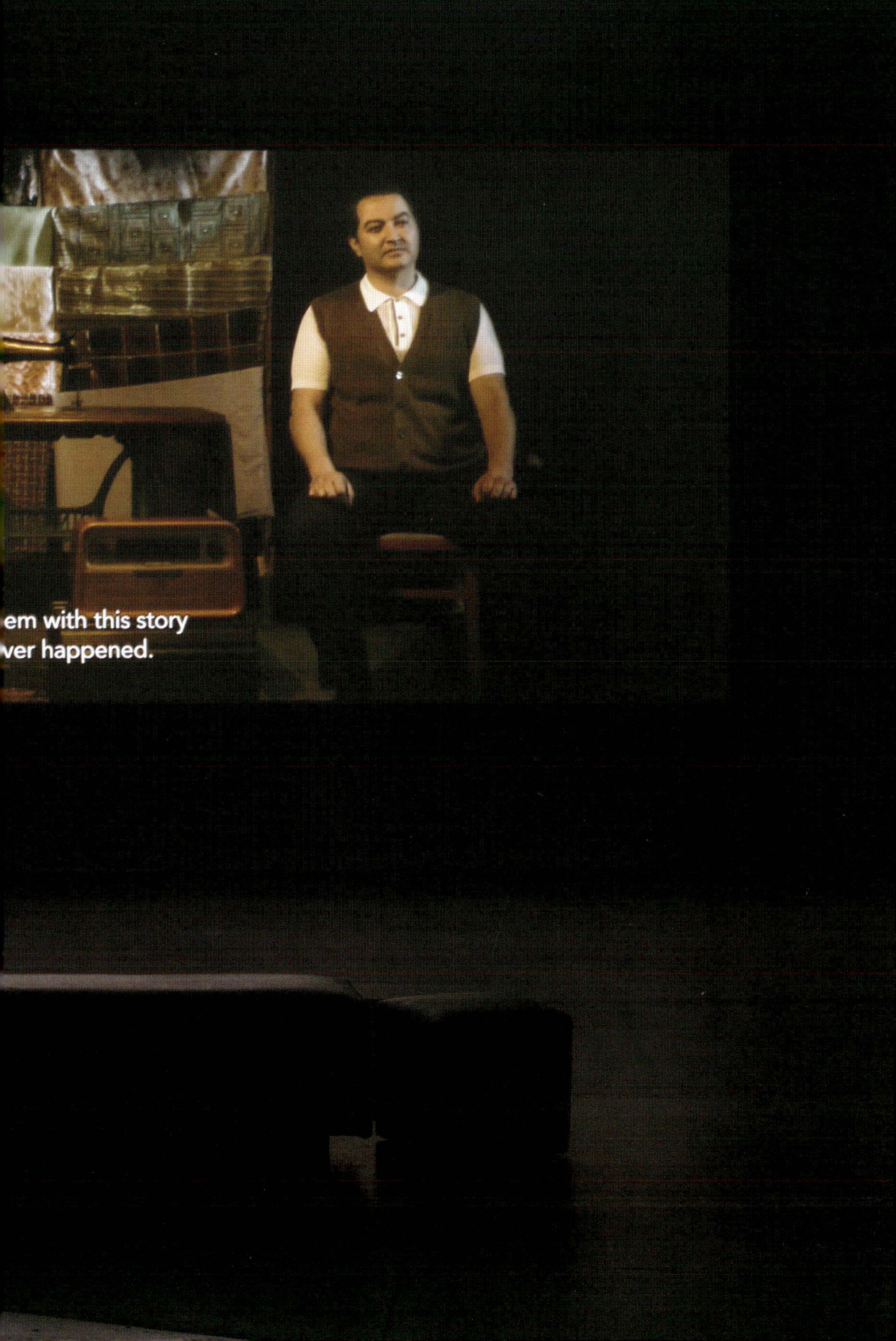
em with this story
ver happened.

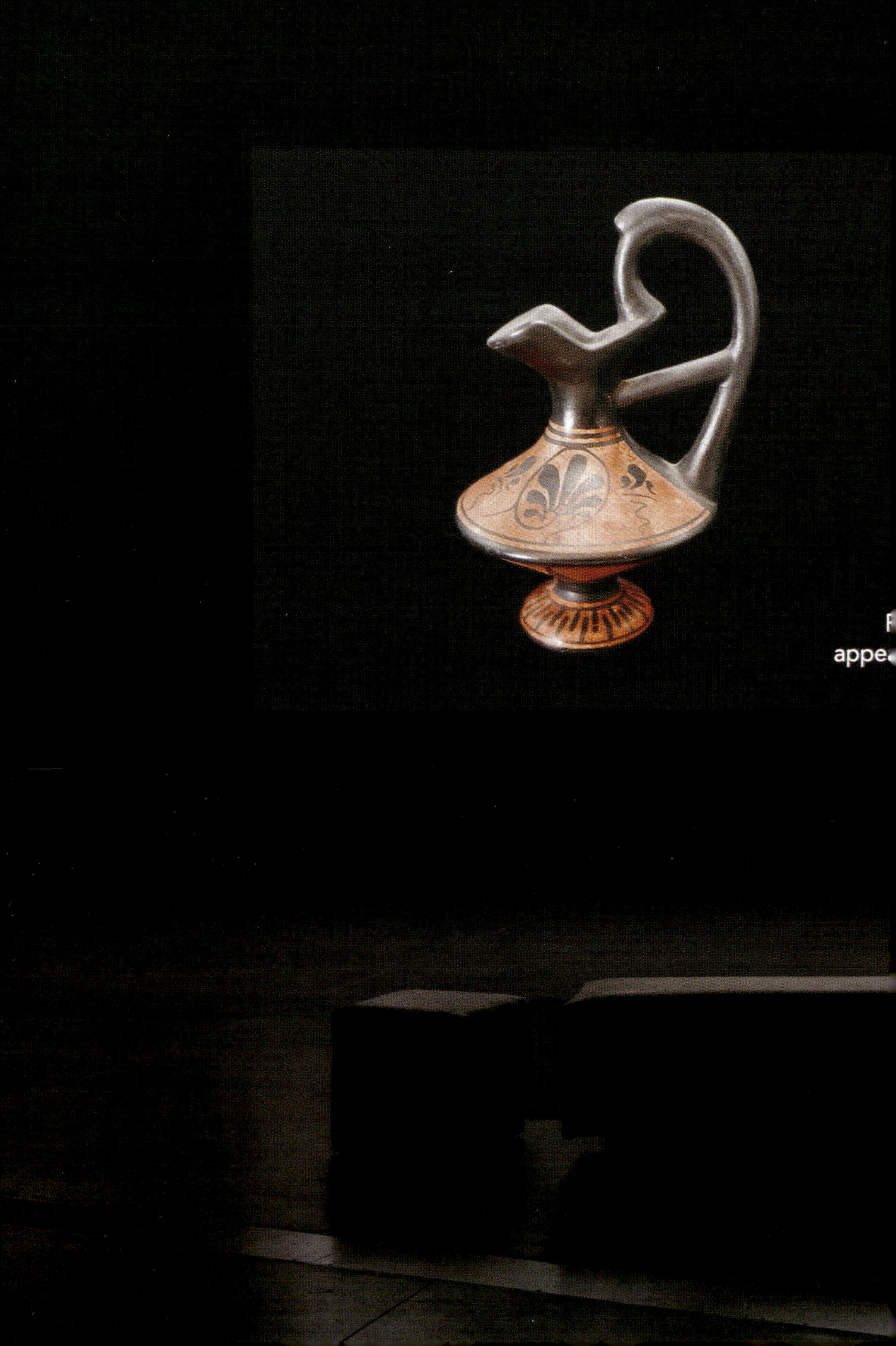

m artefacts
alongside others

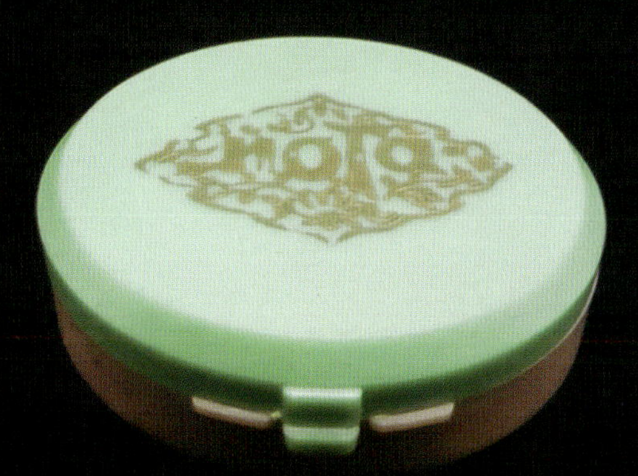

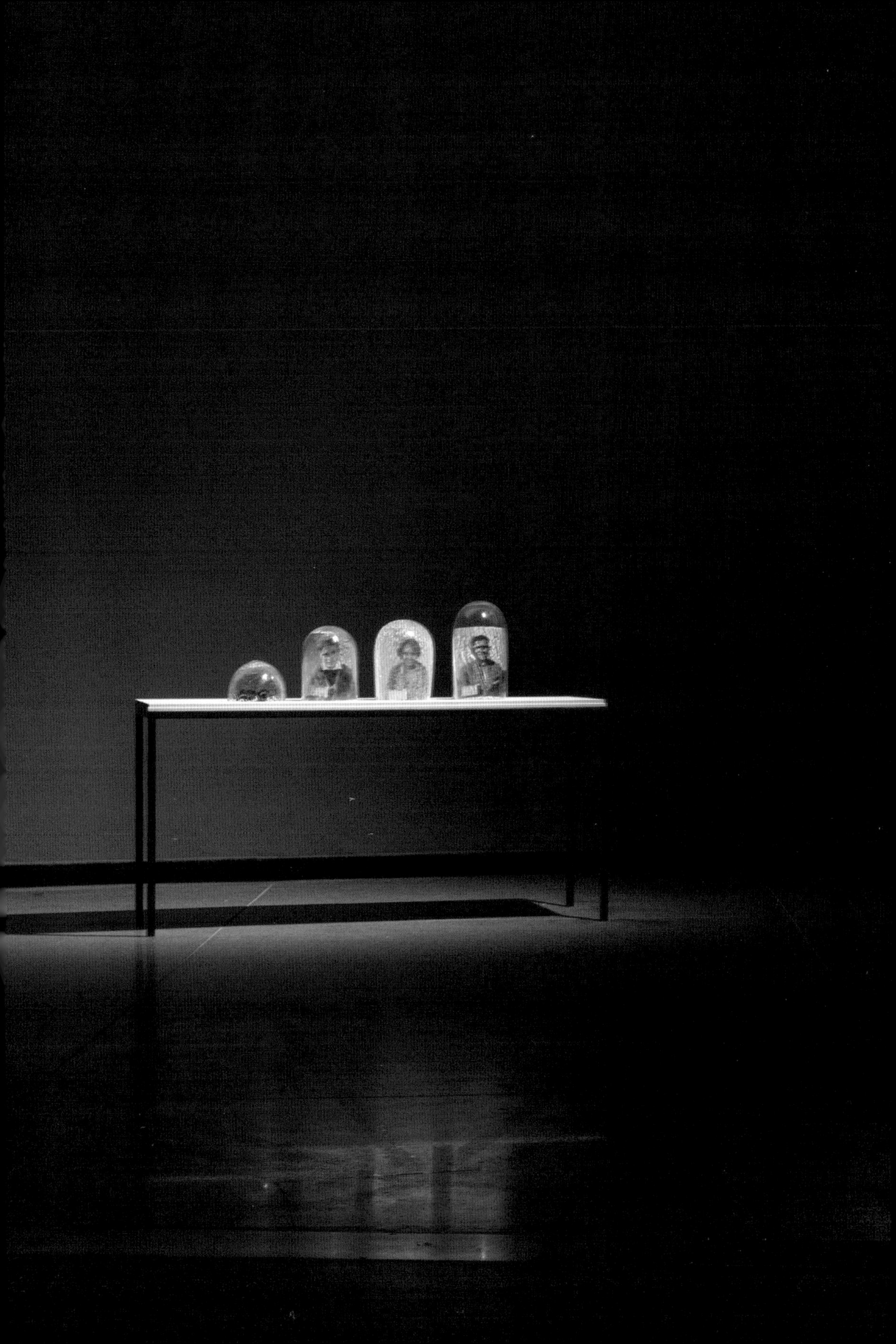

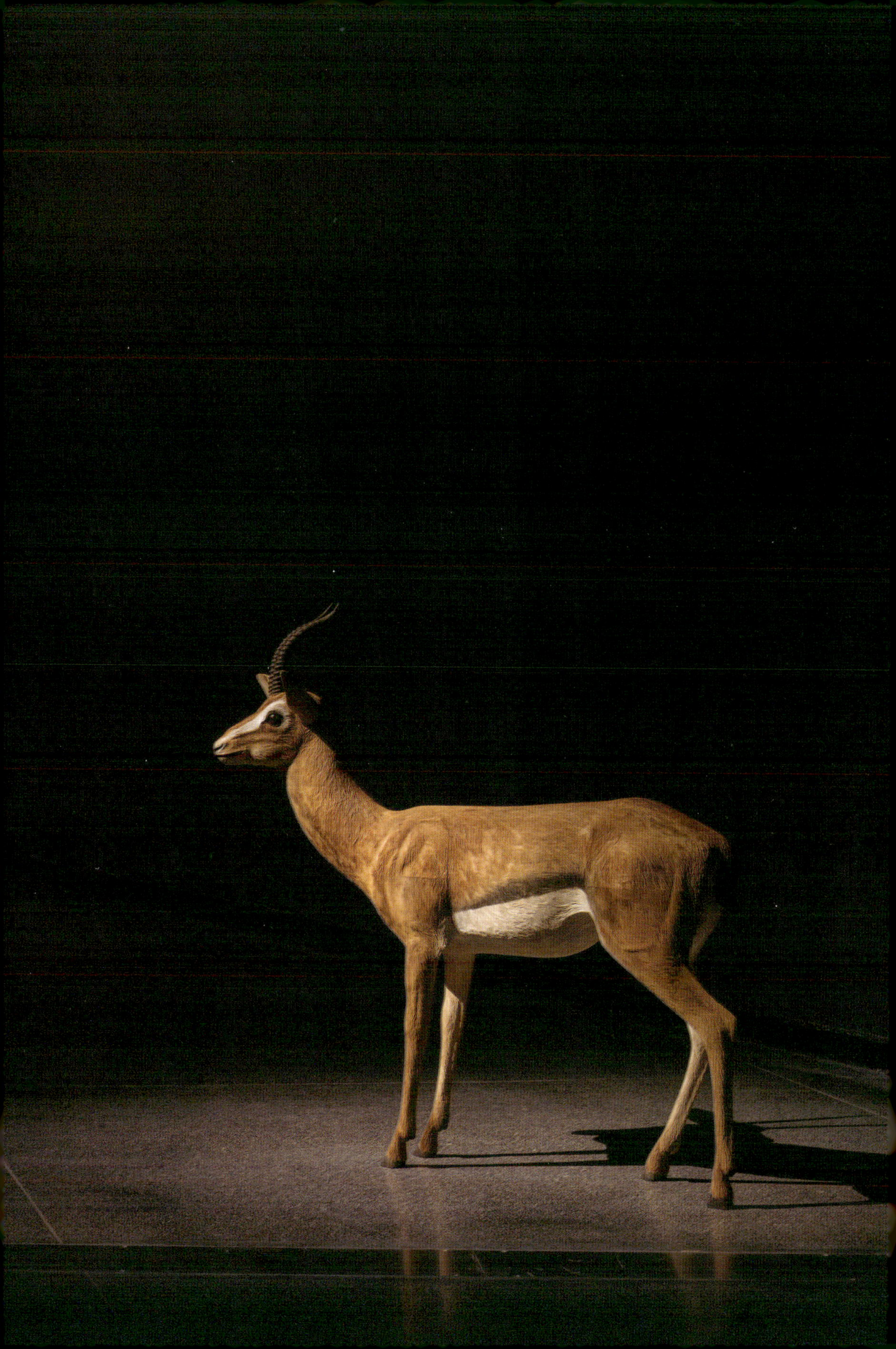

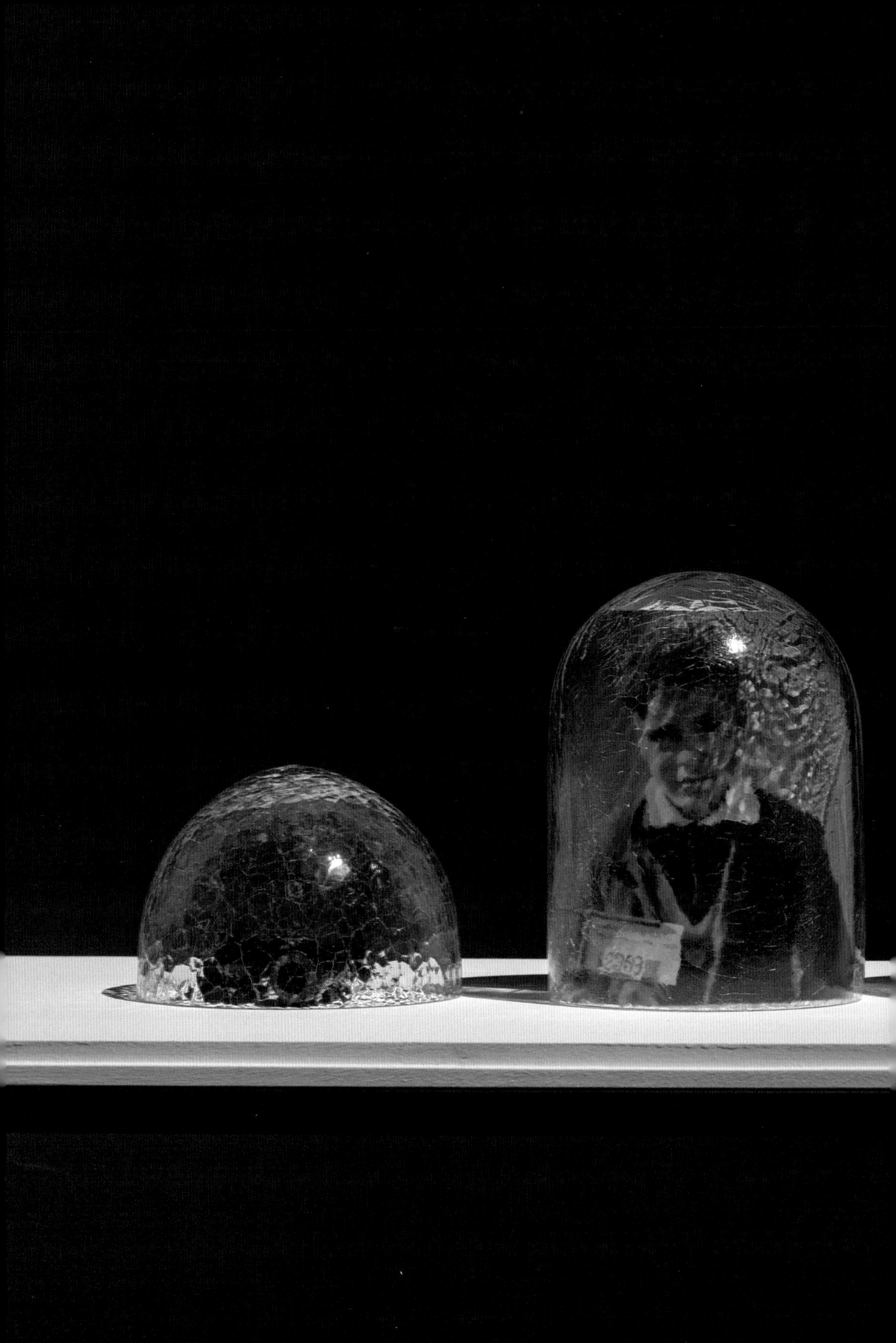

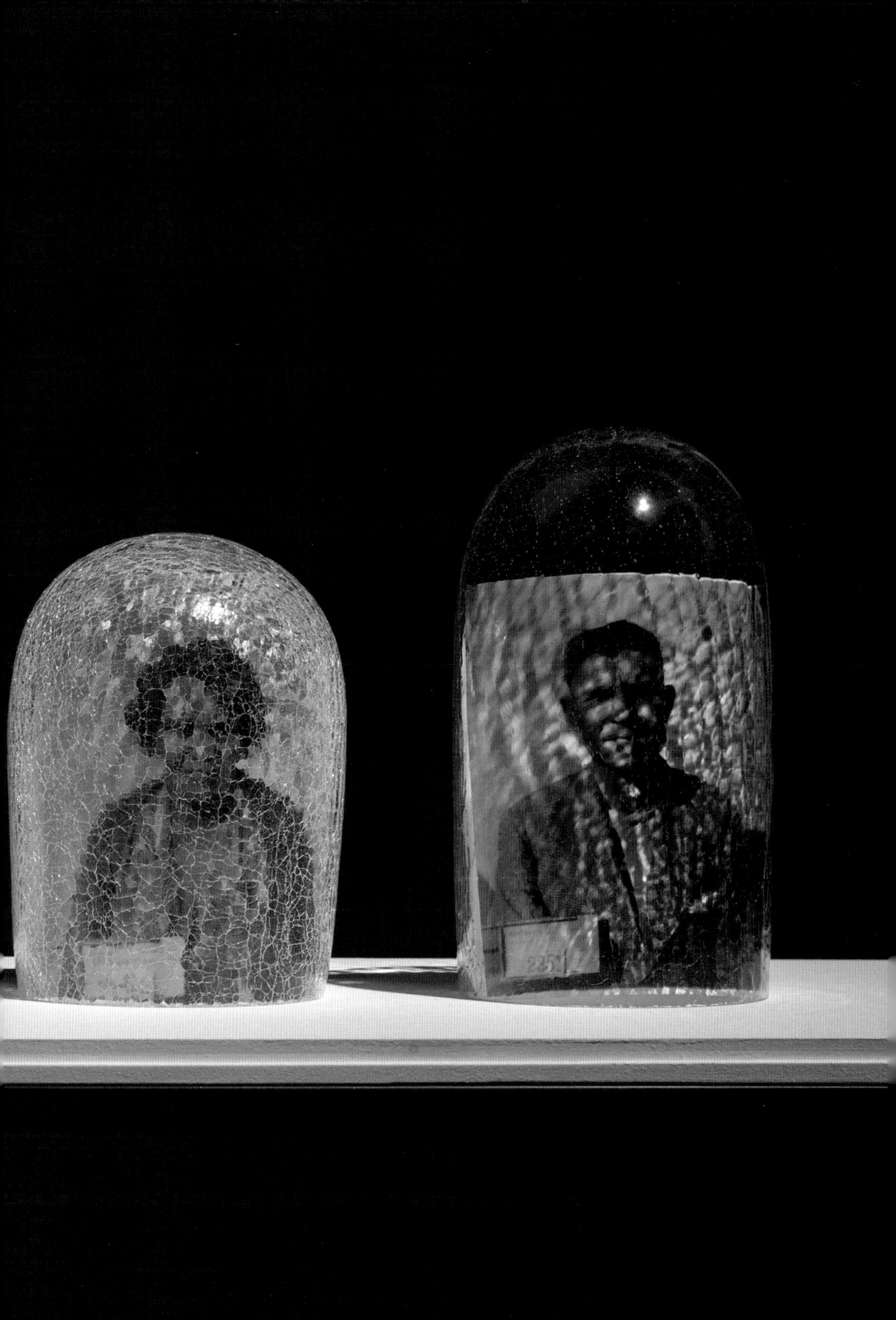

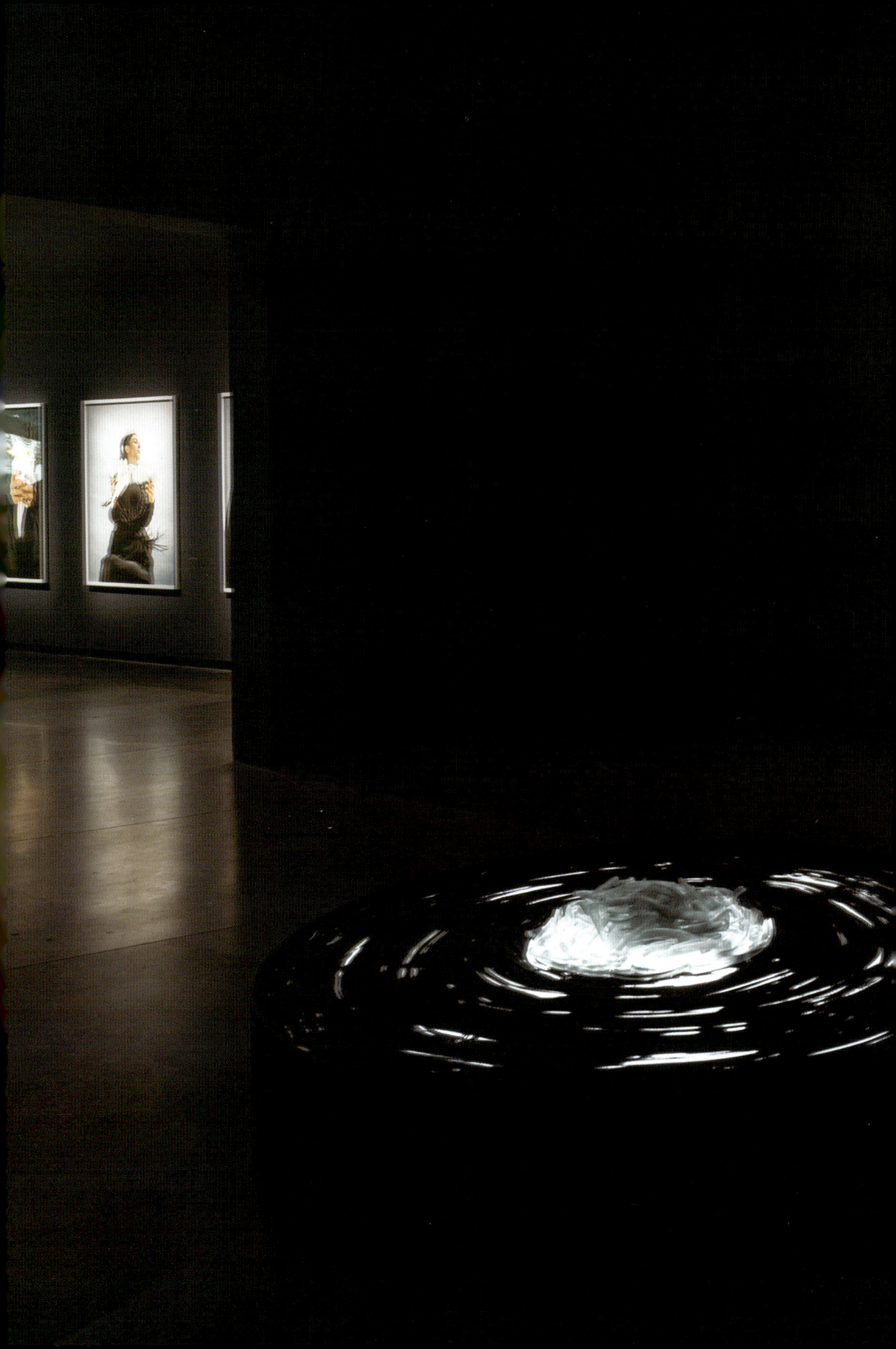

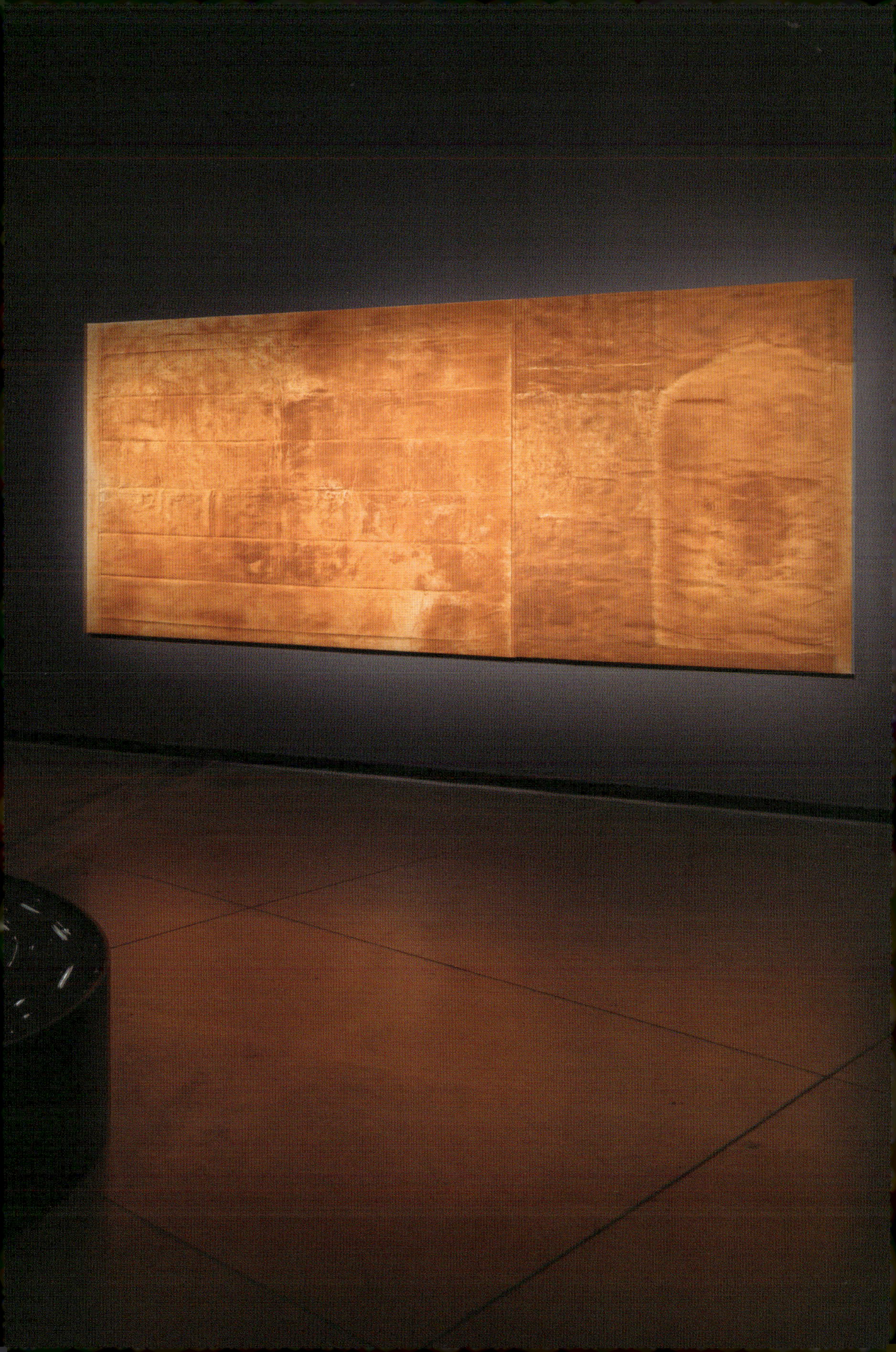

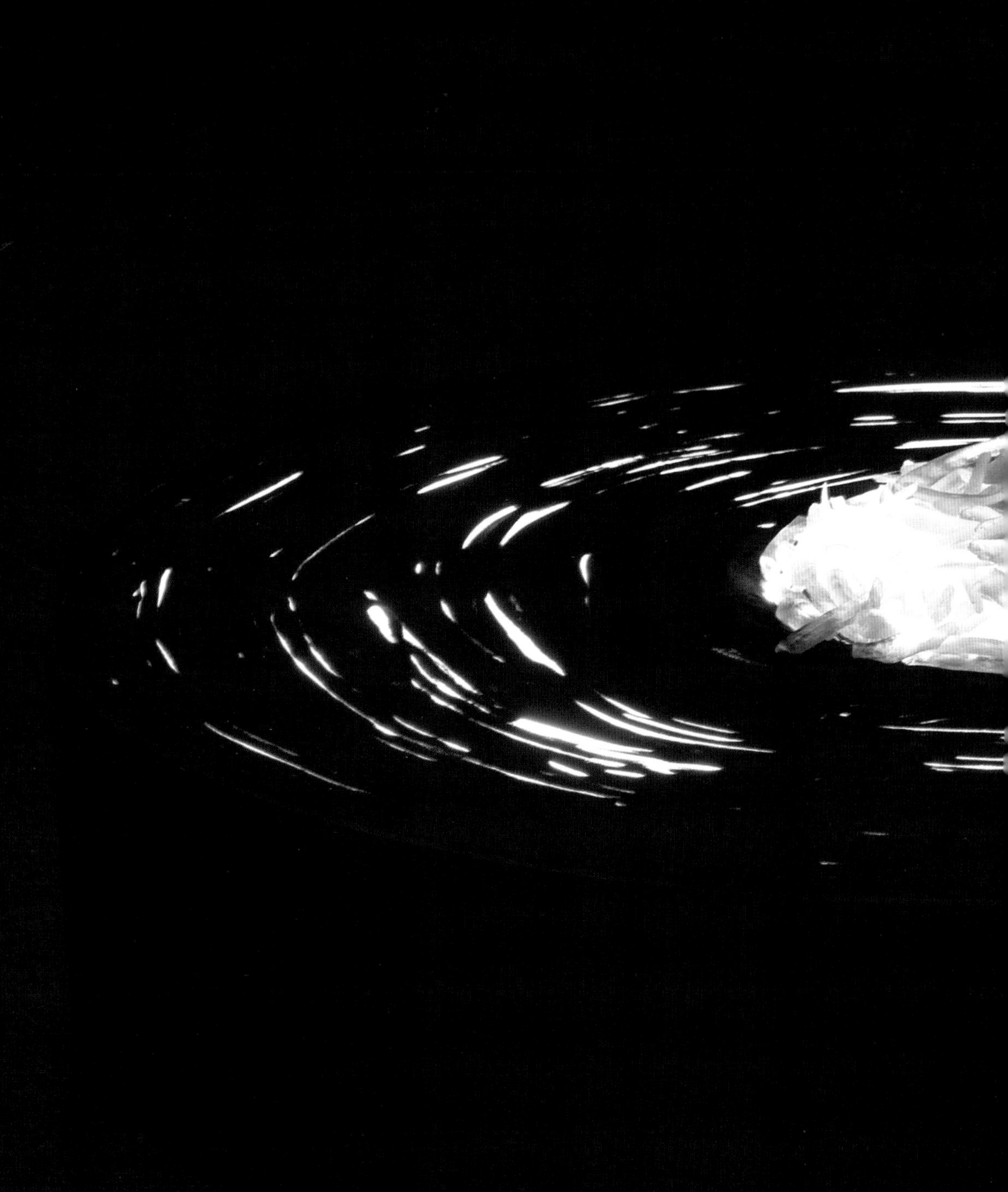

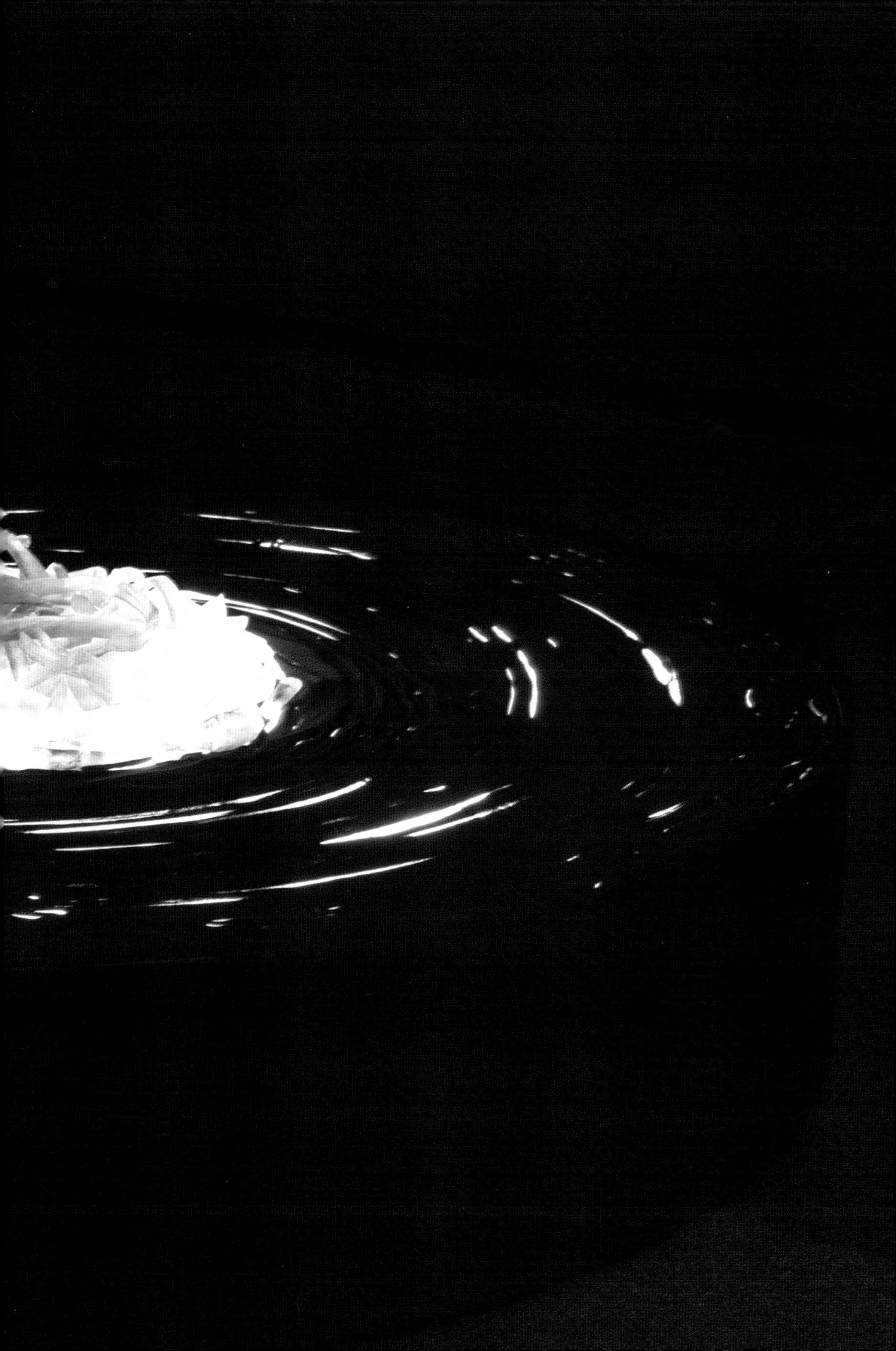

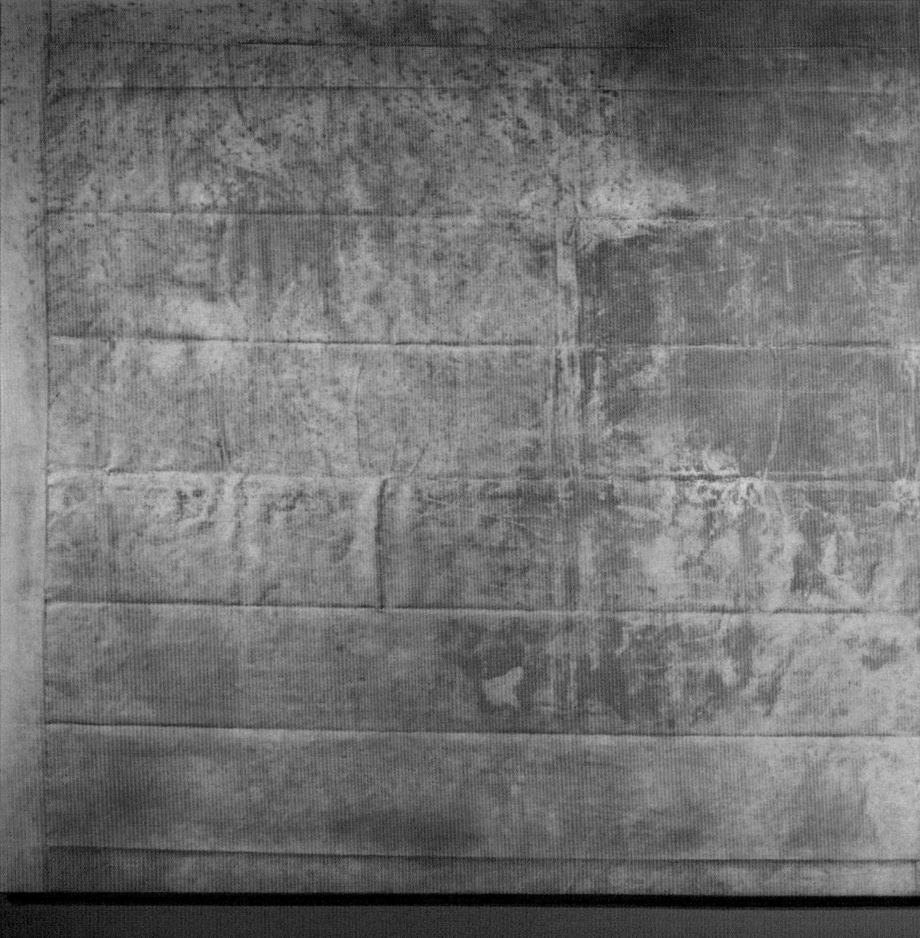

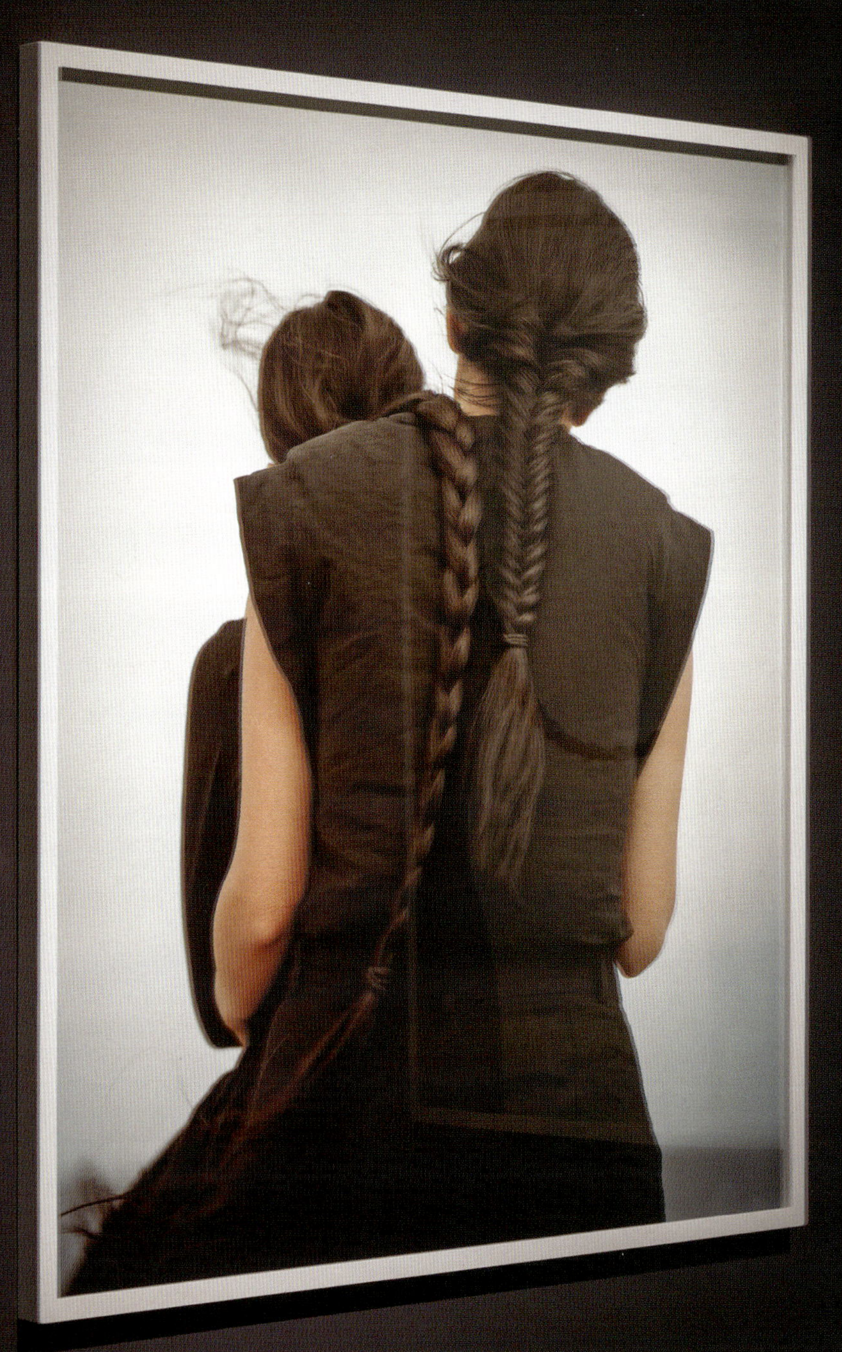

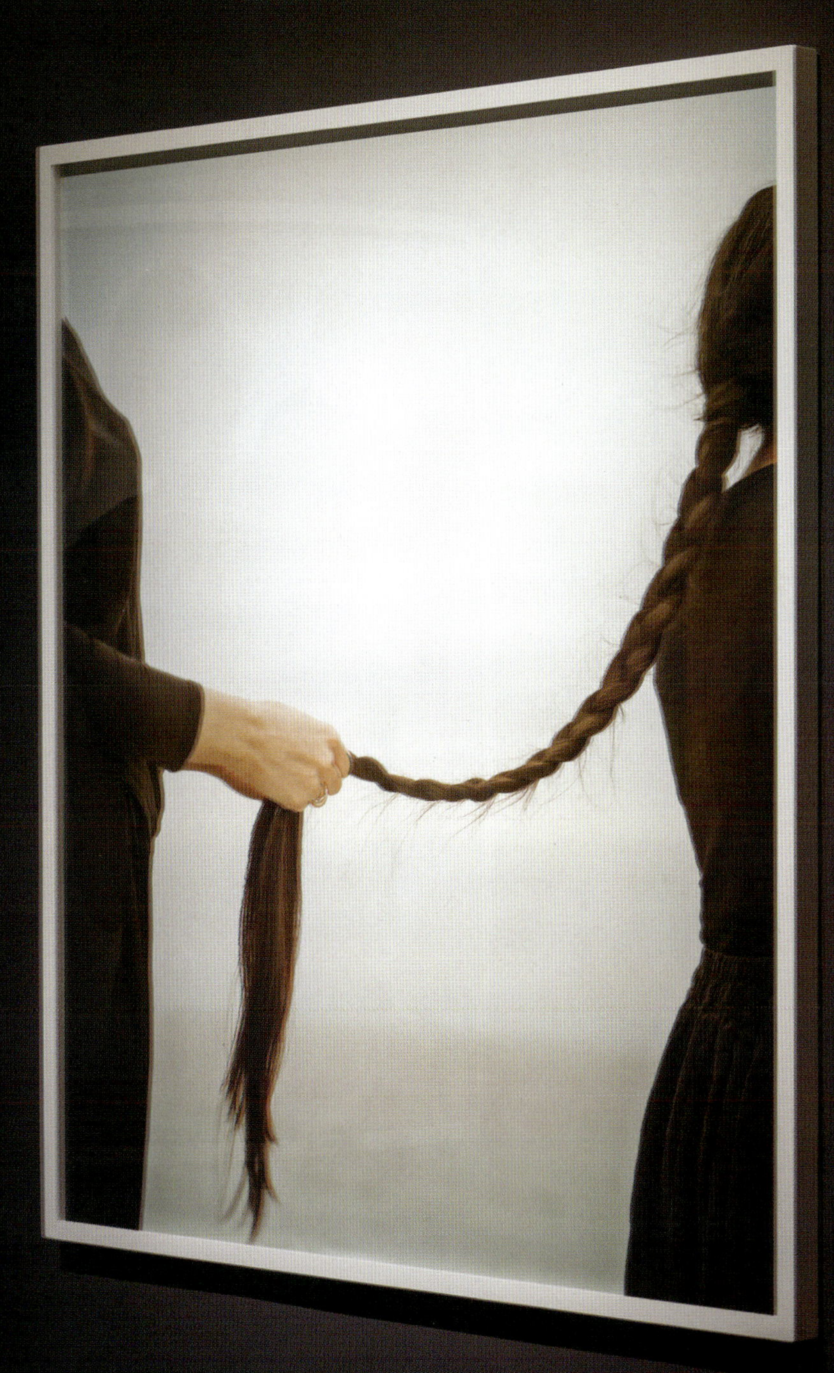

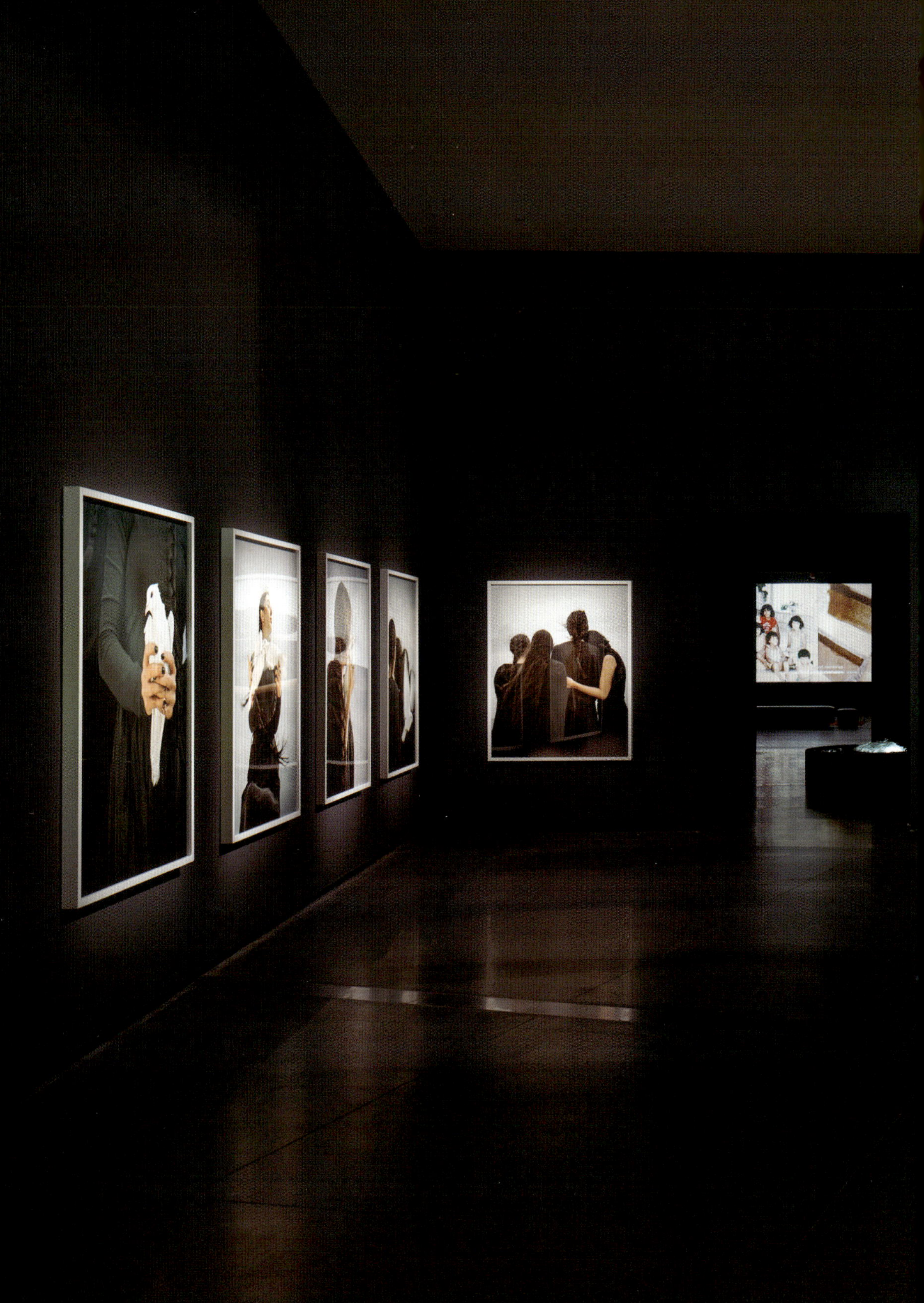

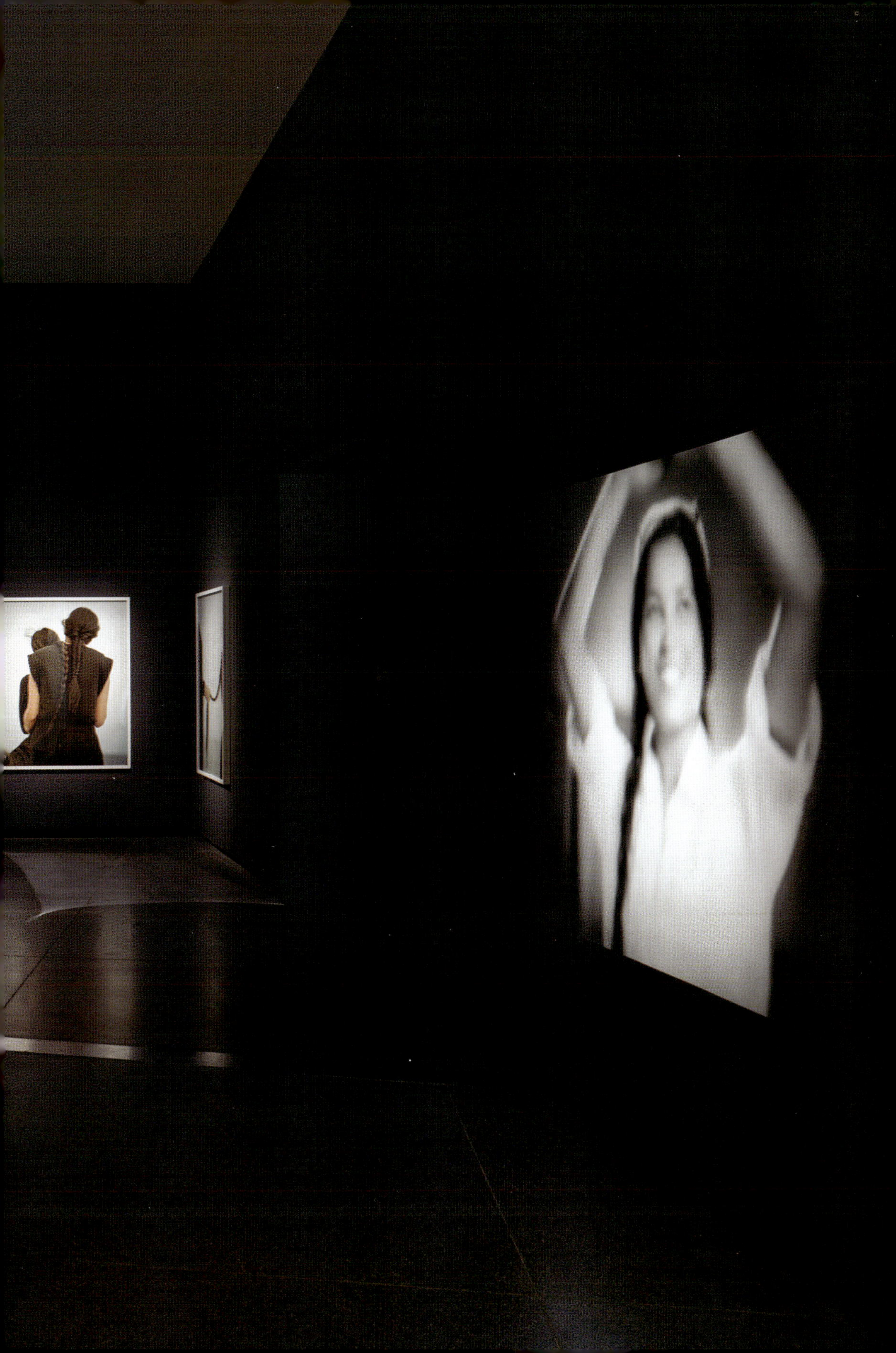

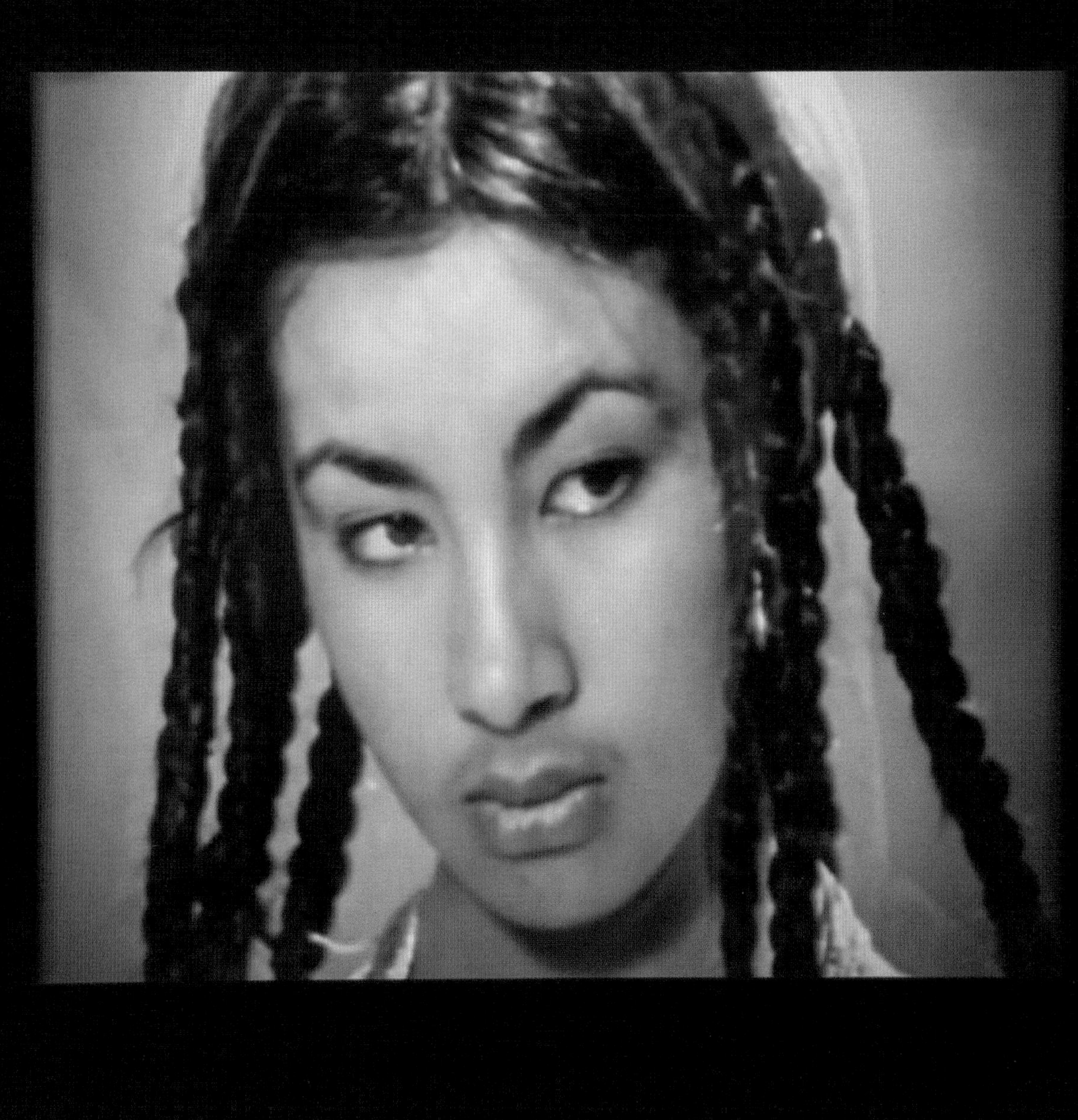

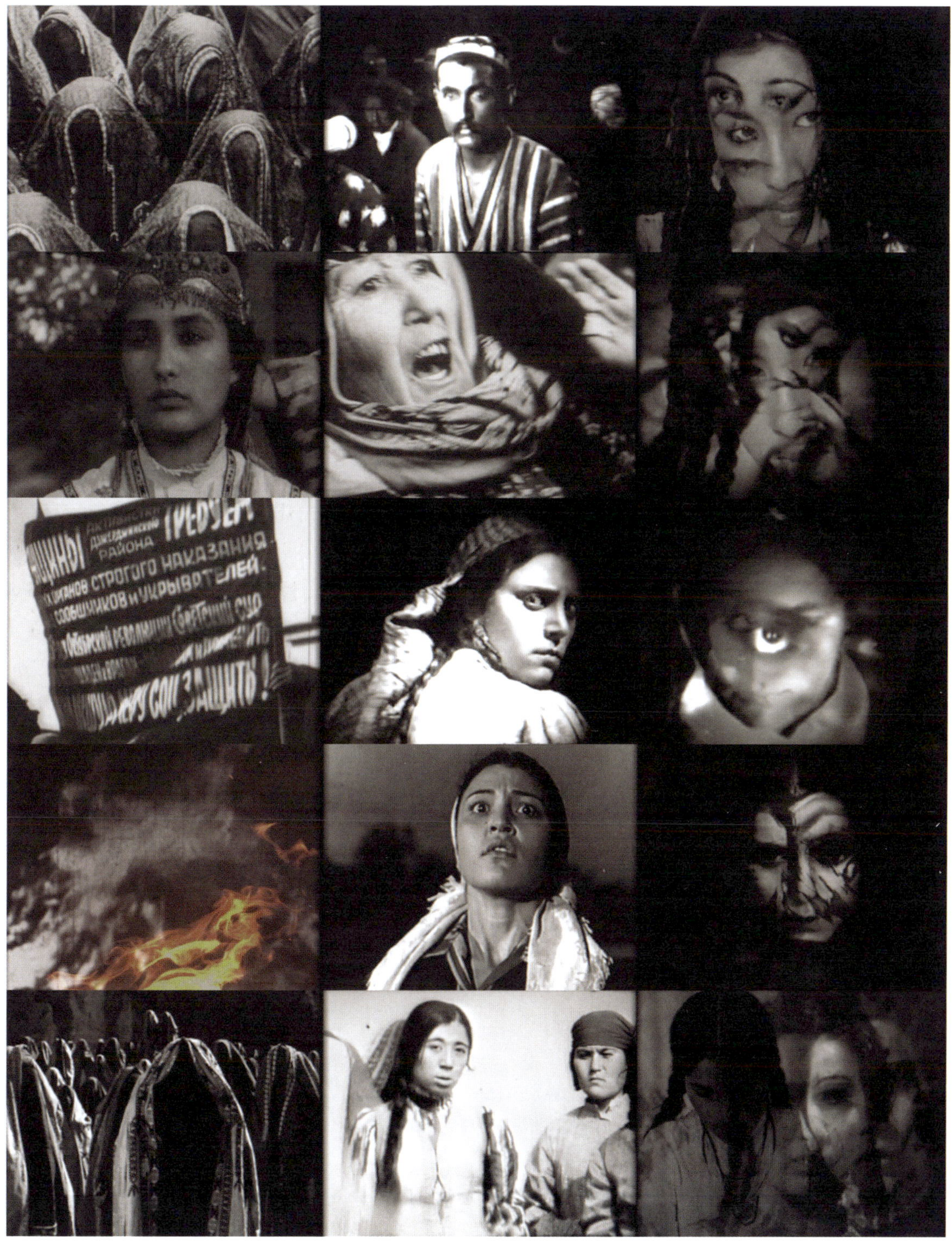

All images: Saodat Ismailova, *Her right* 2020 (still), HD video, 14:00 mins. Supported by Video Jam, UK. Courtesy the artist

Act 1: Resistance

To Resist is to Love
Dr Jessica Clark

‘The land remembers, and so do we’.[1]

Resistance is potent and profound, intimate and intense. It is an expansive act of love that simultaneously moves inward and outward, beyond push and pull notions conjured on the surface.

مقاومة

muqāwama, meaning to oppose; to stand strong.

معارضة

muʿārada, meaning to challenge; to tell truth.

صمود

ṣumūd, meaning determination and resilience.

تحمّل

taḥammul, meaning commitment and endurance.

Across lands, languages and cultures, resistance is deeply nuanced. It is a fierce and generative act of love that is guided by intertwined conceptions of relationality, responsibility and accountability. Boonwurrung, Taungerung, Yorta Yorta, Mutti Mutti and palawa Elder, Uncle Talgium Edwards sums up the heart of resistance, ‘it’s no poor bugger me’.[2]

Whether on the front lines of protest, in the quiet spaces of self-care or through the act of making, resistance emerges from love of self, family, community, and Country. It is a love strong in the face of coloniality, injustice, racism, and intentions to deceive or erase. It is a love that bleeds and believes.

Ngāti Awa and Ngāti Porou iwi scholar Linda Tuhiwai-Smith observes that to resist is to, ‘retrench in the margins, retrieve what we were, and remake ourselves’, so that ‘spaces of marginalisation’, might become spaces for connection and collectivity.[3] To resist is to love urgently, to understand what is at stake: past, present and future.

Resistance is a love that leans into uncomfortability—it is vulnerable, it is brave, and it doesn't shy away from the hard conversations. American author and theorist bell hooks notes, 'true resistance begins with people confronting pain... and wanting to do something to change it'.[4] Resistance is love made actionable; it chooses hope.

This act of love runs deep. It is engrained in breathing and being. This embodied nature of resistance is poetically conveyed through Dr Nur Shkembi's curation of *Five Acts of Love*, as a form of love that manifests in human action and in Country.[5] It is a love that tethers the local and the global, the self with the world, and attests the interdependency and interconnection of all things.

Resistance as love lives in ceremony, in protest, in creativity and community. It is a love that ripples through the body, in memory and the spirit. It is a love alive through the sharing of knowledge, in turning-up and speaking-out, and in being open to new points of connection in a world designed to divide.

Resistance as love seeks and stands for truth. It nurtures the continuation of culture, and cares for Country. It advocates for the safety, security and self-determination of people and place. It protects what is sacred, sovereign and true, and calls for the re-storying and revisioning of histories.

Resistance as love acknowledges the strength and resilience of those who have come before us, and those who have fought for us. It is an act of love for us—for our families, for our communities, for humanity—and for those who will come after us.

It is joy *and* pain.

It is the strength within *and* collective action.

It is survivance *and* solidarity.

In the words of Yoorook Justice Commission Deputy

Chair, and Kerrupmara and Gunditjmara man, Travis Lovett, at his recent Long Walk for Truth address, 'the silence ends here'.[6]

Resistance is a radical act of love for self, for one another and for the future. Larrakia, Tiwi, Chinese Malaysian and Muslim writer Dr Eugenia Flynn explains, it is a love found in 'light, it is deep, it is personal, and it is expansive'.[7] Resistance as love holds steadfast in the belief that transformation is possible, and urges a deeper, better and kinder way forward, together.

'Let this manifestation of love resist and rise to the top'.[8]

1. Travis Lovett, Yoorook Justice Commission Deputy Chair, *Walk for Truth to Parliament*, address, Naarm/Melbourne, 18 June, 2025.
2. Talgium Edwards, personal communication with author, 21 February 2025.
3. Linda Tuhiwai-Smith, *Decolonizing Methodologies: Research and Indigenous Peoples*, 2nd ed., Zed Books, London, 2021, pp. 3-4.
4. bell hooks, *Yearning: Race, Gender, and Cultural Politic*, South End Press, Boston, 1999, p. xi.
5. Dr Nur Shkembi, *Five Acts of Love*, Exhibition Summary, 2025.
6. Travis Lovett, Yoorook Justice Commission Deputy Chair, *Walk for Truth to Parliament*, address, Naarm/Melbourne, 18 June, 2025.
7. Eugenia Flynn, *Five Acts of Love*, Artist Statement, 2025.
8. Ibid.

Act 2: Revolution

for love of country
Dr Eugenia Flynn

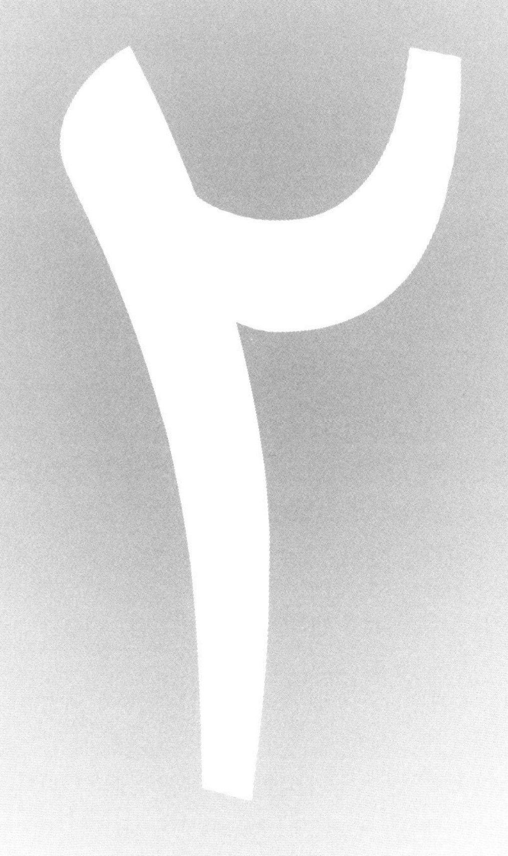

REVOLUTION AGAINST OLD MATE AT THE RSL AND OTHER ACTS OF REVOLUTIONARY LOVE

I spot him before he actually notices me. Old Mate is drunk and belligerent, not minding his own business like the other men, an older group drinking socially together at the RSL's bar. They glance up, a bit surprised to see us in *their space*, but nonetheless return to their drinks and conversation without further acknowledgement. Years of minding my safety as a visibly Asian woman in Australia, as an Aboriginal woman living within the legacy of colonialism, I am quick and experienced in surveying my surroundings in public spaces. I look out for white men like this one, especially when they have been drinking. I sit with my husband, visibly Aboriginal, and my sister, she looks Asian just like me. On edge now, I go to order food and broaden my Australian accent when speaking to bistro staff; move my body with a bravado that I hope mimics masculine arrogance. Let me be clear: this is a coping strategy that I do not encourage others to emulate. Born out of a response to an environment of racist sexism, it is a disguise I have adopted, increasingly so, since I started wearing the hijab.

My accent and my adopted male swagger can do nothing to help me today. Old Mate is circling our table, looking at me, holding his beer, staggering back and forth from the bar to the bistro and muttering under his breath. My husband and my sister are not yet aware, but I can sense what is coming; I keep looking at him nervously, unwittingly encouraging the confrontation.

Then, Old Mate tells me repeatedly to remove my hijab.

The relationship between patriotism, nationalism, war, racism and xenophobia—a relationship that reaches its pinnacle within the traditions of ANZAC Day—is one that fascinates me. Perhaps because my father was in the Army Reserves during the Vietnam War, or because my grandfather died during the bombing of Darwin, or maybe because several of my uncles served in various wars for

Australia. When Old Mate will not leave me alone at the RSL, I invoke my family's history because I know he cannot possibly conceive that this non-white Muslim woman is 'Australian', that she has a right to be sitting in the RSL in her hijab. I do so, not as a point of nationalist pride, but purely and simply to make him leave me alone. To feel safe again. To give him a bit of righteous comeuppance while in the process of politely telling him to *fuck off*.

Despite my family legacy, I have mostly felt exclusion from the ANZAC legend and mythology as an institution of white patriarchy within Australian society. Scholar Fiona Nicoll writes that in the development of the ANZAC legend, the male digger face was presented as 'a vital component...that linked national identity to the supremacy of the Caucasian race'.[1] Of course, there have been recent attempts to make the ANZAC tradition more inclusive. Ngaanyatjarra musician Vonda Last's song 'For Love of Country' pays 'tribute to the Aboriginal and Torres Strait Islander men and women who served their country, and in many cases sacrificed their lives, at a time when they weren't recognised as citizens of Australia'.[2] A form of resistance to white patriarchal nationalism, songs such as Last's seek to create space for *our* histories.

Through reflecting upon my textual practice of resistance to racist and xenophobic nationalism, I have been pushed to think more about revolution. That is, to push beyond resistance and *into* revolution. Revolution against Old Mate at the RSL, revolution as writer, revolution as textual practice of resistance. Here, my revolution is decolonising the word 'country' toward Aboriginal ways of understanding land and 'Country'. Here, my revolution is reclaiming the phrase 'for love of country' and playing with words toward other light and loving forms such as Country music, beloved by Aboriginal peoples across the continent; Sacred Country, as understood by Aboriginal people as the land where we bury our dead and by me as the place where I prostrate my head in prayer as a Muslim; Countrymen, as the term used by Aboriginal people to describe those from amongst their kin/clan/tribe/language group; and Country as living entity that claims us as Aboriginal people, with our Aunties and Uncles as sovereign custodians of the land.

For me, Country is loving. Revolution is loving. At a time when there are multiple ongoing armed conflicts around the world, when the world is being drawn further and further toward an outbreak of global war, what could be more revolutionary than a call to alternative versions of the phrase 'for love of country'?

1. Fiona Nicoll, *From Diggers to Drag Queens: Configurations of Australian National Identity*, Pluto Press, Sydney, 2001, p. 113.
2. See Radio National Breakfast, *For Love of Country: Shining a spotlight on Indigenous wartime contributions*, https://www.abc.net.au/listen/programs/radionational-breakfast/shining-a-spotlight-on-indigenous-wartime-contributions/9695490, accessed 3 July 2025.

for
love
of
Country

a capital 'C'
and all that this
means

for
love
of
country
...music

the one who loves it,
and the one who
loves me

for
love
of
Sacred
Country

where the bodies of
the dead are laid to
rest

where I gently place
my forehead in
prayer

my nose, my palms,
my toes, my knees

my *Sacred Country*

for
love
of
Countrymen

who live in deep
culture,
covered in ochre and
covered in earth

for
love
of
Country

love to the Aunties
and the Uncles who
welcome us

love to the land
which claims us

love to the ones who
sove-reign supreme

Act 3: Intimacy

A Dictionary of Intimacy
Sara M Saleh

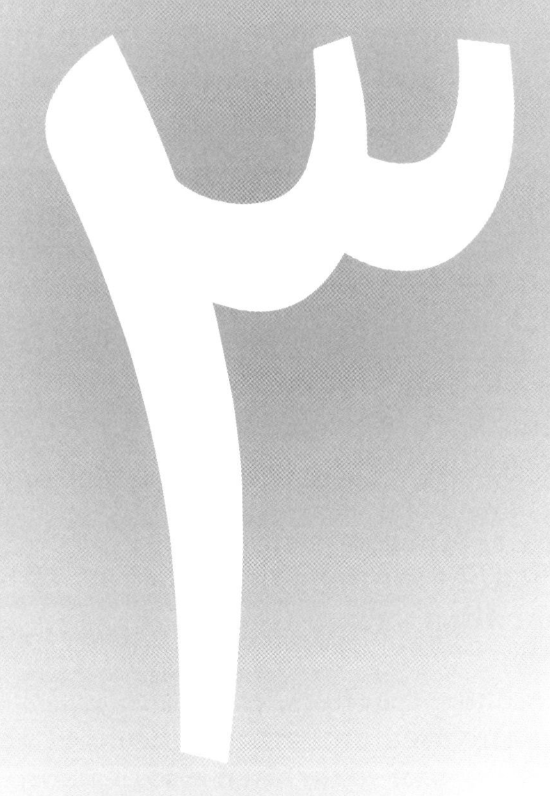

This is a dictionary of selected entries that offers not only a poetic taxonomy of closeness, but a political, spiritual, and embodied reorientation of how we define intimacy itself. This is a vocabulary collapsing under the weight of grief, forged in mourning and memory, where love insists on itself ...

And we—despite the many terrible things—believe it.

1. The Intimacy of Language

To be Arab, to be Muslim, demands a personal, sacred relationship with language.

Language has long been our site of struggle and sanctuary. Our literature holds what history erases: fracture, longing, unspeakability. The Qur'an is poetry embodied—a living language that sings and submits, even silence is meaningful.

I believe literature is the only channel capable of holding all the paradoxes and impossibilities of our existence—and still remain preserved.

2. The Intimacy of Ritual/Return

Ritual teaches slowness. It reclaims our time from the churn of capitalism and hyperproduction.

Like a sacred tawaf, we circle toward presence. It is not about performance, but practice. Not control, but communion. Ritual reminds us that care—of self, of spirit, of kin—is amanah, a sacred trust.

Of course, there are teachers, frameworks, rituals and rules—they are the mechanism. But none of that can dictate the contours of your own relationship with God. The portal is within. The return is always inward. That is the rationale.

3. The Intimacy of Rage

Rage is often gendered, pathologised, dismissed. But righteous rage—is not the opposite of love—it is its fiercest form. The kind birthed from harm, from witnessing, from truth-telling—it is edifying.

To refuse silence, to reject civility and decorum, to insist: justice is not negotiable. To burn together, to scheme toward liberation—this too is intimacy.

4. The Intimacy of Self-Love

Self-love is abolitionist. It is the undoing of ego, the nafs, the uprooting of carceral logic within. It asks: how do I hold myself? How do I refuse harm, even in how I disagree?

In this moment, when we are being called to recalibrate our lives and purpose, our relationship with self is a rehearsal for how we move in the world, with others. Some healing only arrives through sincere connection. The kind that frees us. From callousness. From mindless consumption. From capitalist self-neglect. Toward care. Toward collective abundance.

It teaches us a deeper, messier, fuller self-love.

5. The Intimacy of Uprising

Empire records what it deems central. And erases those it finds inconvenient.

But resistance remembers. It is the backs of comrades, the fists of women, the rocks of the displaced, that re-centre the story, that refocuses those who have no place in canon.

Our fractured selves belong here. This is where we can exist.

6. The Intimacy of Kin-Making

Love beyond state-sanctioned scripts is survival. Kin-making is to radically reshape the world on our own terms.

Mobbed by the freedom fighters, the survivors of fracture and fragmentation, those who consider themselves on the fringes of 'mainstream'. We share spaces where we can bring all parts of ourselves, anchored in an understanding that our struggles are related, an extension of each other.

We gather not just for strategy, but for building futurities. These entanglements are not metaphor. They are method. They are movement.

We must stretch the imagination—beyond binaries of individual versus collective—toward a porous, relational, kinship that transcends limited neoliberal conceptions of settler time and settler love.

7. The Intimacy of 'Endings'

What if the ending isn't collapse, but compost? What if the end is not absence, but an opening? A threshold?

Some endings—like dispossession, exile, death— are not endings at all, but invitations to reimagine continuity.

Endings mean: To Mourn, To Mark, To Begin again. Intimacy lives here too.

Act 4: Memory

A Journey to Kandahar
Elyas Alavi

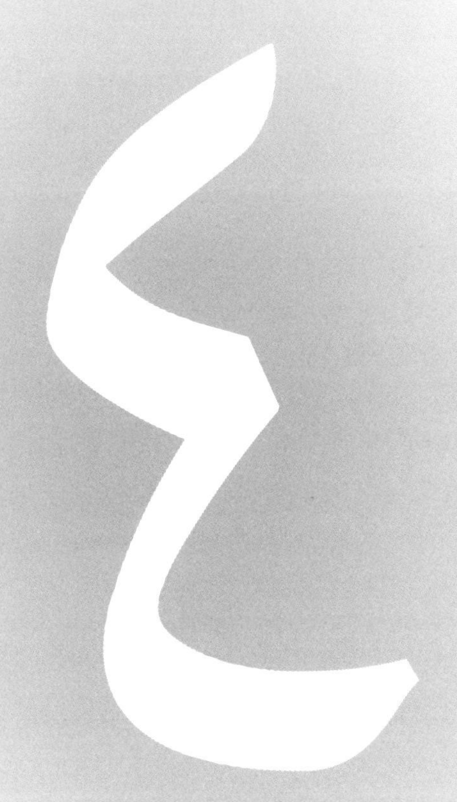

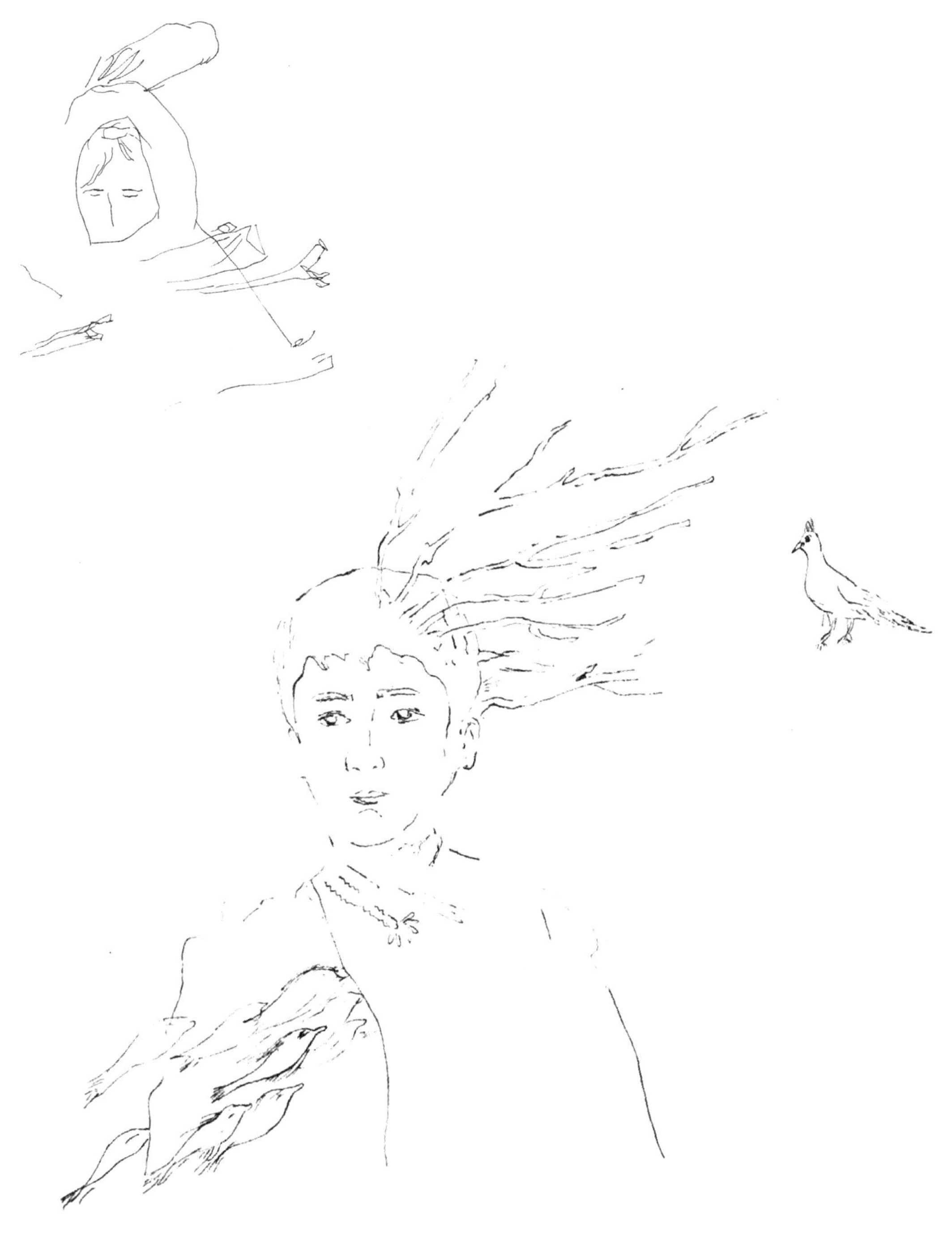

Elyas Alavi, drawing from *Another Kind* series, 2025, pen on paper.

We hugged each other tightly
and quickly let go.
With no hope of seeing each other we cried:
"Hope to see you soon."
Grandma laughed:
"Surely this isn't a journey to Kandahar?"
And we, too, smiled bitter, bitter smiles.

Then
The train's whistle blew, mournfully
A thousand yearning travellers waved from that side
A thousand yearning friends waved from this side.

We went home
And sought refuge in the dark rooms
Grandmother
Threw her arms around the porch
Took one look at the blossoms in the orchard
And loudly, loudly sobbed.

Note: "A journey to Kandahar" is a Persian idiom for a long, difficult journey. There is an additional level of irony here because for Afghans, a journey could well be a journey to Kandahar, although this one is not.

The poem translated from Farsi/Persian into English by Dr. Zuzanna Olszewska.

سفر قندهار

یکدیگر را در آغوش گرفتیم تنگ
و تُند رها شدیم
بی امیدِ دیدار فریاد زدیم:
"به امید دیدار"
مادرکلان خندیده گفت:
"سفر قندهار است مگر؟"
ما نیز تلخ تلخ لبخند زدیم.

آنگاه
قطار آهي کشید، جگرخون
هزار مسافر دلتنگ از آن طرف دست تکان دادن
هزار یار دلتنگ از این طرف دست تکان دادند.

به خانه آمدیم
و به اتاق‌هاي تاریك پناه بردیم
مادرکلان
دست در گردن ایوان انداخت
به شکوفه‌هاي باغچه نگاهي کرد
و بلند بلند گریست.

Act 5: Annihilation

Fanaa
Dr Safdar Ahmed

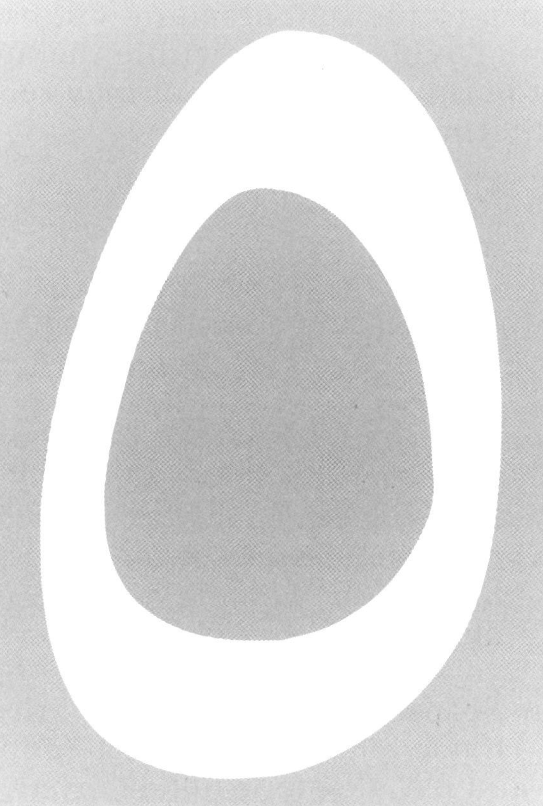

Fanaa is a profound and fertile concept in Islamic mysticism. Usually translated into English as 'annihilation', it describes a moment of self-dissolution—when the ego is effaced and absorbed into God or the Divine Reality.

This concept is extrapolated from Qur'anic verses describing the permanence of God and perishability of every created thing: 'All that lives on earth or in the heavens is bound to pass away: but forever will abide thy Sustainer's Self, full of majesty and glory' (55:26–27).[1]

In mystical writing *fanaa* is often paired with *baqā*, which denotes a return to the self, albeit now subsisting in the Divine—the Divine abiding within the human being. These are not permanent states but may recur many times over a lifetime.

Rābiʿa al-Baṣrī (713–801) framed this experience of self-loss as an awakening of the heart, explaining: 'The wakeful heart is the one that has lost itself in the real (Divine Reality/ *al-ḥaqq*). When someone is lost, what has he to do with a friend? Extinction in God (*fanaa*) is here'.[2]

At a glance, the notion of *fanaa* may seem paradoxical—suggesting that beneath the self lies a kind of no-self. Seen differently, it appears elusive in loosening the distinction between creation and its Divine source. Some have found the apparent conflation of humanity with God—and its expression by human lips—implicitly heretical.[3]

But this is to misconstrue Sufism's imaginative approach to the human–Divine relationship, which mobilises contradiction and paradox to facilitate mystical insights. In their descriptions of the spiritual path, Sufi writings often play upon the binaries that structure religious thought. These include the distinctions between sacred and worldly realms, the external world and its hidden reality, collective religious practices (*sharīʿah*) and the subjective spiritual path (*ṭarīqah*). Yet all of this yields to what I think is Sufism's most important and overriding characteristic:

the focus on Divine Love as the locus of creation, and the force by which all dualities—opposition, separation, and selfhood—are overcome.

The *ḥadīth* of the Hidden Treasure—'I was a hidden treasure and loved to be known'—says that God created the world in order to be recognised. Ibn 'Arabi (1165–1240) interpreted this to mean creation is a continuous process of Divine self-disclosure which is grounded in the experience and recognition of love:

> None but God is loved in existent things. It is God who is manifest within every beloved to the eye of every lover—and there is nothing which is not a lover. So all the cosmos is a lover and beloved, and all of it goes back to God.[4]

Ibn 'Arabi went on to analogise worldly, romantic love with the mystical yearning for a Divine Beloved.[5] The conceptual tension between these forms of love is beautifully explored in volumes of Sufi poetry, where complex urges towards things temporal and eternal, worldly and otherworldly, lofty and low desires, are so often intertwined.

Here I will argue for a concept of *fanaa* which is not located solely in the realm of private mystical experience. Islam does not offer a quietist, atomised, capitalist version of 'spirituality' that promotes internal calm as a means of coping with—rather than challenging—the political status quo.

For the anti-colonial South Asian poet and philosopher, Muhammad Iqbal (1877–1938), Islam advocates for empowerment: activating the self as a dynamic force—not in the moment of its dissolution but at the point of its worldly subsistence *(baqā')*. Iqbal held that to merge with the Divine without returning to reshape the world would render impossible both spiritual fulfillment and the realisation of Islam's movement committed to principles of justice. Writing in the early twentieth century, he decried Western materialism, race-based nationalism and the imperial-capitalist system it sustained.[6]

This prompts us to consider the contemporary implications of *fanaa* within a theology of Divine love and worldly return. In a time of genocide, as Israel slaughters tens of thousands of Palestinians in Gaza, how do we subsist? In the fight for a vision of moral justice, actions grounded in the communal values of shared commitment and sacrifice (and not the glory-seeking ego) seem more important than ever.

Perhaps there is no incongruity between spiritual pursuits and the mundane yet consequential choices that shape our daily lives. We must return to a world in pain—upset, clear eyed, enraged by the horrors that surround us—yet always subsisting in love.

1. Muhammad Asad, trans., *The Message of the Qur'an*, Dar al-Andalus, Gibraltar, 1980, 55:26–27.
2. Michael Anthony Sells and Carl W. Ernst, *Early Islamic Mysticism: Sufi, Qur'an, Mi'raj, Poetic and Theological Writings*, Paulist Press, New York, 1996, pp. 163–64. For Rabia's focus on the heart as metaphor, see also Rkia Elaroui Cornell, *Rabi'a: From Narrative to Myth—The Many Faces of Islam's Most Famous Woman Saint, Rabi'a al-'Adawiyya*, Bloomsbury Academic, London, 2019, chapter. 4.
3. The most well-known example of this is the ecstatic statement of Manṣūr al-Ḥallāj (858–922), who proclaimed *'Anā al-Ḥaqq'* ('I am the Divine Real'). al-Hallāj was ultimately executed by Abbasid authorities—a decision that may have stemmed as much from political causes as from perceptions of heretical incarnation. Whatever the case, his famous utterance is now commonly associated with heresy in the popular imagination and Sufi practitioners have rarely engaged in such outlandish expressions. See Carl W. Ernst, 'Shath,' in *Encyclopaedia of Islam*, 2nd ed., vol. 9, Brill, Leiden, 1997, pp. 361–62.
4. Henry Corbin, Creative Imagination in the Sufism of Ibn 'Arabī, Routledge, London, 1969, p. 114.
5. Sa'diyya Shaikh, *Sufi Narratives of Intimacy: Ibn 'Arabi*, Gender, and Sexuality, University of Minnesota Press, Minneapolis, 2012.
6. Muhammad Iqbal, *Thoughts and Reflections of Iqbal*, ed. Syed Abdul Vahid, Sh. Muhammad Ashraf, Lahore, 1964, p. 244.

List of works

ABDUL-RAHMAN
ABDULLAH
Pretty Beach 2019
painted wood, silver plated
ballchain, crystals
500.0 x 500.0 x 500.0 cm
Created on Bindjareb
Nyoongar Country
Private collection, Sydney NSW
Courtesy the artist

Witness 2025
painted wood, horn, glass eyes
110.0 x 37.0 x 107.0 cm
Created on Bindjareb
Nyoongar Country
Acknowledgment: Department
of Local Government, Sports &
Cultural Industries, WA
Courtesy the artist and Moore
Contemporary, Perth

HODA AFSHAR
Untitled #5, #7, #1, #3, #6, #2, #4
(from *In turn* series) 2023
framed photographic print
165.0 x 132.0 cm (each)
Created on Wurundjeri Country
Courtesy the artist and Milani
Gallery, Meanjin/Brisbane

MEGAN COPE
The tide waits for no-one 2020-21
250 kiln cast TV glass, yungan/
dugong bones and Minjerribah
mineral sand, plinth, lightbox
40.0 x 200.0 (diam) cm (overall)
Created on Bundjalung Country
Courtesy the artist and Milani
Gallery, Meanjin/Brisbane

EUGENIA FLYNN
for love of country 2025
ink on paper
size variable
Created on Boonwurrung Country
Courtesy the artist

D HARDING
She come from the low-country, he come from the high-country II 2025
earth pigments and acrylic on linen
left panel: Ghungalu red soil and
acrylic binder
right panel: Bidjara red soil and
acrylic binder
181.0 x 390.5 cm (2 panels).
Created on Turrbal and
Yuggera Country
Courtesy the artist and Milani
Gallery, Meanjin/Brisbane

SAODAT ISMAILOVA
Her right 2020
HD Video
14:00 mins
Supported by Video Jam, UK
Courtesy the artist

KHALED SABSABI
At the speed of light 2016
11 channel HD video sculpture
installation, audio, 25 x 4 gold leaf
/ acrylic and enamel paint work on
photographic paper, 5 multilingual
text panels on paper
dimensions variable
individual monitor labels
SPEED OF VIDEO
SEQUENCES (R-L) as pictured
on p. 34–35
Stage 1 – Video duration 218hrs 34mins 28secs – Speed at 381 metres per second; Stage 2 – Video duration 54hrs 23mins 32secs – Speed at 1,531.021888341879 metres per second; Stage 3 – Video duration 13hrs 35mins 54secs – Speed at 6,123.962454549169 metres per second; Stage 4 – Video duration 3hrs 23mins 59secs – Speed at 24,494.84908897786 metres per second; Stage 5 – Video duration 51mins – Speed at 97,971.39150326797 metres per second; Stage 6 – Video duration 12mins 45secs – Speed at 391,885.5660130719 metres per second; Stage 7 – Video duration 3mins 12secs – Speed at 1,561,419.052083333 metres per second; Stage 8 – Video

duration 48secs – Speed at 6,245,676.208333333 metres per second; Stage 9 – Video duration 12secs – Speed at 24,982,704.83333333 metres per second; Stage 10 – Video duration 3secs – Speed at 99,930,819.33333333 metres per second; Stage 11 – Video duration 1sec – Speed at 299,792,458 metres per second.
Created on Dharug and Dharawal Country
Courtesy the artist and Milani Gallery, Meanjin/Brisbane

LARISSA SANSOUR & SØREN LIND
Familiar Phantoms 2023
film
42:00 mins
Courtesy the artists

YHONNIE SCARCE
N000, N2359, N2351, N2402 2014
blown glass, archive photographs
dimensions variable
Created on Wurundjeri Country
Courtesy the artist and THIS IS NO FANTASY, Naarm/Melbourne
Collection of Darebin Art Collection

ALI TAHAYORI
Archive of longing 2024-25
Selected works from series:
Untitled #1, Untitled #3, Untitled #10b, Untitled #13, Untitled #18, Untitled #19, Untitled #21, Untitled #22 & #26, Untitled #24, Untitled #25, Untitled #27, Untitled #28, Untitled #29, Untitled #30, Untitled #31 (Maman Simin), Untitled #33, Untitled #34b, Untitled #35, Untitled #37, Untitled #41, Untitled #42 (They/Them), Untitled #43 (FAGS), Untitled #45, Untitled #46, Untitled #47, Untitled #48, Untitled #49 & #50, Untitled #52, Untitled #54, Untitled #55, Untitled #56 (Descend)
UV print on glass, hand-cut glass, silicone on aluminium
dimensions variable
Created on Gadigal and Darug Country
Courtesy the artist and THIS IS NO FANTASY, Naarm/Melbourne

Sisterhood 2021
pigment ink-jet print, collage
120.0 x 120.0 cm
created on Gadigal and Dharug Country
Courtesy the artist and THIS IS NO FANTASY, Naarm/Melbourne

HOSSEIN VALAMANESH
The lover circles his own heart 1993, (Paris edition 2017)
silk, modal and electric motor, controller, support structure and wire
190.0 x 190.0 cm
Created on Kaurna Country
Collection the artist estate
Courtesy the artist and Angela Valamanesh

In praise of the beloved 2006
almonds, false eyelashes on paper
29.5 x 21.0 x 1.5 cm
AP (unique edition of 7)
Created on Kaurna Country
Collection Abdul-Rahman Abdullah
Courtesy the artist and Angela Valamanesh

INSTALLATION VIEWS

33 Hossein Valamanesh, *In praise of the beloved* 2006

34-35 Khaled Sabsabi, *At the speed of light* 2016 (detail)

36-37 Khaled Sabsabi, *At the speed of light* 2016, installation view

38-39 Khaled Sabsabi, *At the speed of light* 2016 (detail)

40-41 *Five Acts of Love*, installation view

42-45 Ali Tahayori, *Archive of longing* 2024-25, installation view

46-47 Ali Tahayori, *Archive of longing* 2024-25 (detail)

48-49 *Five Acts of Love*, installation view

50 Abdul-Rahman Abdullah, *Pretty Beach* 2019 (detail)

51 Abdul-Rahman Abdullah, *Pretty Beach* 2019, installation view

52-53 Abdul-Rahman Abdullah, *Pretty Beach* 2019 (detail)

54-55 *Five Acts of Love*, installation view

56-57 Hossein Valamanesh, *The lover circles his own heart* 1993 (Paris edition 2017), installation view

58-59 *Five Acts of Love*, installation view

60-63 Larissa Sansour & Søren Lind, *Familiar Phantoms* 2023, installation view

64-65 *Five Acts of Love*, installation view

66-67 Yhonnie Scarce, *N000, N2359, N2351, N2402 2014*, installation view

68-69 *Five Acts of Love*, installation view

70-71 Eugenia Flynn, *for love of country* 2025, installation view

72-73 Megan Cope, *The tide waits for no-one* 2020-21, installation view

74-75 D Harding, *She come from the low-country, he come from the high-country II* 2025, installation view

76-77 (L-R) Hoda Afshar, *Untitled #2, #4* (from In turn series) 2023, installation view

78-79 *Five Acts of Love*, installation view

80 Saodat Ismailova, *Her right* 2020 (still), installation view

Cover (Front, internal fold and back): Hossein Valamanesh, *The lover circles his own heart* 1993 (Paris edition 2017)

Inside front cover: Saodat Ismailova, *Her right* 2020 (still)

Inside back cover: Saodat Ismailova, *Her right* 2020 (still)

2-3 D Harding, *She come from the low-country, he come from the high-country II* 2025 (detail)

Biographies

ABDUL-RAHMAN ABDULLAH

born 1977, Dharawal Country, Port Kembla, NSW
lives and works on Bindjareb Nyoongar Country, WA

Abdul-Rahman Abdullah is an artist based on Bindjareb Nyoongar Country, on a cattle farm in the Peel region of Western Australia. Working primarily in sculpture and installation, he explores the intersections of identity, culture, and the natural world. Living and working in an agricultural setting, his practice offers alternative perspectives that traverse diverse—and often disparate—communities. At the core of his artistic approach is the lived connectivity of family.

A 2012 graduate of Curtin University, Abdullah's major project highlights include *WA Focus* at the Art Gallery of Western Australia, 2015; the *Adelaide Biennial* at the Art Gallery of South Australia, 2016 and 2022; *Dark Horizons* at the Pataka Art + Museum, New Zealand, 2017; *The National* at the Museum of Contemporary Art, Sydney, 2019; *Everything Is True* at the John Curtin Gallery, 2021; *Land Abounds* at Ngununggula, 2022; and the Uchiboso Arts Festival, Japan 2024.

He has served as a board member of the Perth Institute of Contemporary Arts, 2017–21, a council member of the National Gallery of Australia, 2023–24, and is the ongoing set designer for Marrugeku, 2019–present.

Abdul-Rahman Abdullah is represented by Moore Contemporary, Boorloo/Perth.

HODA AFSHAR

born 1983, Tehran, Iran
lives and works on Wurundjeri Country, Naarm/Melbourne VIC

Hoda Afshar was born in Tehran, Iran, in 1983, and is currently based in Melbourne, Australia. She holds a Bachelor of Fine Art in Photography from Tehran and completed a PhD in Creative Arts at Curtin University.

Working at the intersection of conceptual, staged, and documentary image-making, Afshar's practice examines the representation of gender, marginality, and displacement. Initially drawn to the documentary image for its potential to reveal hidden truths, she is equally invested in interrogating the complicity between photography and systems of power. Informed by her personal experience of migration and cultural dislocation, her work uses the camera's inherent intrusiveness as a point of departure to explore the relationships among truth, image, and authority—while simultaneously challenging traditional conventions of image-making.

Afshar's work is held in numerous public and institutional collections, including the Victoria and Albert Museum, London; Kadist Collection, Paris; the National Gallery of Victoria, Melbourne; the Art Gallery of South Australia, Adelaide; the Auckland University Art Collection, Auckland; the Monash University Museum of Art, Melbourne; and the Art Gallery of New South Wales, Sydney.

Hoda Afshar is represented by Milani Gallery, Meanjin/Brisbane.

MEGAN COPE

born 1982, Meanjin/Brisbane QLD
lives and works between Minjerribah and Bundjalung Country QLD

Megan Cope is a Quandamooka artist from Moreton Bay/ Minjerribah (North Stradbroke Island). Her multidisciplinary practice—including site-specific sculptural installations, video works, and painting—investigates the entangled legacies of colonial histories, environmental change, and mapping practices.

Cope's recent solo exhibitions include *Whispers* at the Sydney Opera House, 2023, and *Fractures and Frequencies* at UNSW Galleries, Sydney, 2021. Her work has been featured in major international group exhibitions such as *Sharjah Biennial 16*, United Arab Emirates; *Hawai'i Triennial 25: Aloha Nō*, Honolulu, 2025; *proppaNOW: There Goes the Neighbourhood!* at the Vera List Center for Art and Politics, New York, 2023; *Busan Biennale 2022: We, On the Rising Wave*, South Korea; and *Reclaim the Earth* at Palais de Tokyo, Paris, 2022, among others.

A member of the renowned Aboriginal art collective proppaNOW—recipients of the 2022–24 Jane Lombard Prize for Art and Social Justice—Cope has received numerous accolades, including the Creative Australia Award for Emerging and Experimental Arts, 2024. From 2017 to 2019, she was commissioned as an official Australian War Artist by the Australian War Memorial.

Megan Cope is represented by Milani Gallery, Meanjin/Brisbane.

DR EUGENIA FLYNN

born 1982, Tandanya/Adelaide SA
lives and works Boonwurrung Country, Naarm/Melbourne VIC

Eugenia Flynn is a writer, researcher, and creative whose practice explores narratives of truth, grief, and devastation, interwoven with considerations of race, gender, and identity. Her essays, short stories, and poems have been published in *Hello Keanu! A Poetry Anthology*, *IndigenousX*, *Peril* magazine, *Meanjin*, and *#MeToo: Stories from the Australian Movement*.

Her text-based works have also been featured in visual art exhibitions, including *Waqt al-tagheer: Time of Change* at ACE Open; *Enough* خلص *Khalas: Contemporary Australian Muslim Artists* at UNSW Galleries; and *SOULfury* at Bendigo Art Gallery.

An Aboriginal (Larrakia and Tiwi), Chinese Malaysian, and Muslim woman, Flynn works across her multiple communities to create change through literature, art, community organising, and community engagement. Her practice is grounded in community-driven approaches and critically engaged storytelling across disciplines.

D HARDING

born 1982, Moranbah QLD
lives and works in Meanjin/Brisbane QLD, and internationally

D Harding works across a wide range of media to explore the visual and social languages of their communities as a living cultural continuum. A descendant of the Bidjara, Ghungalu, and Garingbal peoples, Harding draws upon and sustains the spiritual and philosophical sensibilities of their cultural inheritance within the framework of international contemporary art.

Their work is held in numerous significant public collections, including the Tate Modern, London; KADIST, San Francisco/Paris, the Art Institute of Chicago, Griffith University Art Collection, Brisbane; Queensland Art Gallery | Gallery of Modern Art, Brisbane; University of Queensland Art Museum, Brisbane; Museum of Contemporary Art Australia, Sydney; Art Gallery of New South Wales, Sydney; and the National Gallery of Australia, Canberra.

Harding is represented by Milani Gallery, Meanjin/Brisbane.

SAODAT ISMAILOVA

born 1981, Tashkent,
former UzSSR
lives and works in Tashkent and Paris, France

Saodat Ismailova is an Uzbek filmmaker and artist who came of age in the post-Soviet era. Interweaving rituals, myths, and dreams into the fabric of everyday life, her films investigate the historically complex and multilayered cultures of Central Asia. Often grounded in oral storytelling and centered on female protagonists, her work explores systems of knowledge that have been marginalized or suppressed by globalized modernity.

Ismailova studied at the Tashkent State Art Institute and Le Fresnoy—Studio National des Arts Contemporains, France, and maintains an artistic practice between Paris and Tashkent. In 2021, she founded the Davra research collective in Central Asia to foster critical dialogue and support the development of the local contemporary art scene.

She participated in both the 59th Venice Biennale and documenta fifteen in 2022, and that same year was awarded the Eye Art & Film Prize in Amsterdam. Her most recent film, *Melted into the Sun*, is featured in the *Nebula* collective exhibition, commissioned by Fondazione In Between Art and Film, during the 2024 Venice Biennale of Art. In 2025 she became a medalist of Art Basel Award, and received a prize from Foundation Pernod Ricard.

KHALED SABSABI

born 1965, Tripoli, Lebanon
lives and works on Gadigal Country, Sydney NSW

Khaled Sabsabi is an acclaimed, award-winning multidisciplinary artist whose practice is grounded in social justice and shaped by his experience of migrating from Lebanon to Australia in 1976 to escape civil war. For Sabsabi, art is a vital tool for communication—a way to engage people through a shared visual language.

Over the past 35 years, he has worked across media, geographical borders, and communities. His early involvement in Western Sydney's hip-hop scene—particularly alongside Arabic, Aboriginal, and Pacific Islander communities—cemented social advocacy as a central tenet of his practice. Sabsabi's work continues to explore ideas of collective humanity while interrogating identity politics and ideological constructs.

His work is held in numerous public and private collections in Australia and internationally. Recent accolades include the Creative Australia Award for Visual Arts, 2023 and the Mordant Family and Creative Australia Affiliated Fellowship in 2024. He has participated in major international biennials, including Sharjah, Sydney, Shanghai, and Marrakech. Khaled Sabsabi, artist, and Michael Dagostino, curator, are the Australian Representatives to the 61st Venice Biennale in 2026.

Khaled Sabsabi is represented by Milani Gallery, Meanjin/Brisbane.

LARISSA SANSOUR

born 1973, East Jerusalem, Palestine
lives and works in London, England

Larissa Sansour is a Palestinian visual artist whose practice engages the intersection of myth, documentary, and historical narrative. Born in East Jerusalem, she studied fine arts in London, New York, and Copenhagen. In 2019, she represented Denmark at the 58th Venice Biennale. Recent solo exhibitions include Amos Rex in Helsinki and Göteborgs Konsthall in Gothenburg.

Sansour frequently employs science fiction as a conceptual framework to explore contemporary social and political realities. While her primary medium is film, her multidisciplinary practice also includes installation, photography, and sculpture. In recent years, her work has focused on themes of nostalgia, memory, and inherited trauma, particularly as they relate to personal and national identity.

SØREN LIND

born 1970, Copenhagen, Denmark
lives and works in London, England

Søren Lind is a Danish author, artist, director, and scriptwriter. With a background in philosophy, he initially wrote books on mind, language, and understanding before shifting his focus to art, film, and fiction. Lind has published novels and short story collections, and his children's books have been translated into several languages.

His films are regularly screened and exhibited at museums, galleries, and film festivals worldwide.

YHONNIE SCARCE

born 1973, Woomera, SA
lives and works Wurundjeri Country, Naarm/Melbourne VIC and Kaurna Country, Tarndanya/Tarndanyangga/Adelaide SA

Yhonnie Scarce was born in Woomera, South Australia, and belongs to the Kokatha and Nukunu peoples. Her interdisciplinary practice spans glass and photography, exploring the political dimensions and aesthetic potential of both mediums.

Scarce's work frequently addresses the enduring impacts of colonisation on Aboriginal communities. Her research has focused particularly on the forced removal and relocation of Aboriginal people from their homelands, as well as the traumatic legacy of the Stolen Generations. Drawing on the strength of her ancestors, Scarce positions herself as a conduit, sharing their stories through her art.

Her work has been collected by major institutions has been commissioned globally including with the Palais de Tokyo, Paris; Tate Modern, London; National Gallery of Australia, Canberra; and The National Gallery of Victoria, Melbourne. Major recent exhibitions include *65,000 Years: A Short History of Australian Art*, Potter Museum of Art, Melbourne, 2025; *Yhonnie Scarce: The Light of Day*, Art Gallery of Western Australia, Perth, 2024; and *Missile Park* at Australian Centre for Contemporary Art, Melbourne, and the Institute of Modern Art, Brisbane in 2021.

Yhonnie Scarce is represented by THIS IS NO FANTASY, Naarm/Melbourne.

ALI TAHAYORI

born 1980, Shiraz, Iran
lives and works on Gadigal Country, Sydney NSW

Ali Tahayori is an Iranian-born Australian artist living and working on Gadigal and Darug lands (Sydney, Australia). He holds a Doctorate in Medicine and a Master of Fine Art in Photomedia from the National Art School, Sydney. Working across photography, installation, and moving image, Tahayori's practice explores queer and diasporic subjectivities, focusing on ideas of home, identity, and belonging from a SWANA (Southwest Asia and North Africa) perspective.

His work frequently incorporates mirrors, glass, and photography, drawing on the traditional Iranian craft of Āine-kārai (آینه‌کاری)—mirrorwork developed by Iranian artisans in the seventeenth century using imported European glass. By combining this historical technique with contemporary materials, text, and imagery, Tahayori creates layered visual experiences that reflect both revelation and concealment

Central to his practice is the experience of being othered, whether through the lens of diaspora or queerness. His kaleidoscopic works draw on ancient Iranian philosophies of light and reflection, offering a poetic interrogation of fractured identity and cultural dislocation.

Ali Tahayori is represented by THIS IS NO FANTASY, Naarm/Melbourne.

HOSSEIN VALAMANESH

born 1949, Tehran, Iran. d. 2022, Tandanya/Adelaide
lived and worked on Kaurna Country, Adelaide SA

Hossein Valamanesh was born in Iran and immigrated to Australia in 1973. He graduated from the South Australian School of Art in 1977 and went on to develop a distinctive multidisciplinary practice that resonated both nationally and internationally. Valamanesh exhibited widely across Australia and abroad, with presentations in Germany, Poland, Japan, Finland, the United Kingdom, Canada, France, and Iran.

His public art commissions include *Knocking from the Inside,* 1989, Adelaide; and *You Just Sit Here...*, part of FARET Tachikawa, 1994, Tokyo. In collaboration with Angela Valamanesh, he created significant works such as *An Gorta Mór,* 1999, a memorial to the Great Irish Famine at Hyde Park Barracks, Sydney; *14 Pieces* on North Terrace, Adelaide; and *Ginkgo Gate*, the western entrance to the Adelaide Botanic Garden. His work *Australia House* was featured in the Echigo-Tsumari Art Triennial, Japan in 2018.

Valamanesh was the recipient of an Australia Council Fellowship in 1998 and undertook a Smithsonian Artist Research Fellowship in Washington, D.C., in 2014. His work is represented in most major Australian public art collections. A major survey of his work was presented at the Art Gallery of South Australia, 2001, and the Museum of Contemporary Art Australia, Sydney, 2002. In 2011, Wakefield Press published *Hossein Valamanesh: Out of Nothingness*, a monograph featuring essays by Mary Knights and Ian North. In 2021–22, a further retrospective, *Hossein Valamanesh: This Will Also Pass*, was held at the Institut des Cultures d'Islam in Paris.

The Estate of Hossein Valamanesh is represented by GAPROJECTS Adelaide, and Grey Noise, Dubai.

CONTRIBUTOR BIOGRAPHIES

DR SAFDAR AHMED
lives and works on Gadigal Country NSW

Safdar Ahmed is an artist, writer, and cultural worker who lives on the traditional lands of the Guringai people. He is a founding member of the community art organisation Refugee Art Project and a member of eleven, a collective of contemporary Muslim Australian artists, curators, and writers. Safdar is the author of *Reform and Modernity in Islam*, IB Tauris, 2013, and the webcomic *Villawood*, which won a Walkley Award in 2015. His graphic novel *Still Alive*, Twelve Panels Press, 2021, won Book of the Year in the 2022 NSW Premier's Literary Awards. Safdar was a participating artist in documenta15, Kassel, Germany, 2022. His latest publication is *The Nightmare Sequence*, UQP, 2025, a collaboration with Omar Sakr.

ELYAS ALAVI
lives and works on Wurundjeri Country VIC

Elyas Alavi is a published poet, and visual artist whose multidisciplinary practice spans painting, sculpture, installation, moving image, poetry, and performance. His work examines the complex intersections of memory, displacement, gender, and sexuality, addressing hyper-invisibilities and challenging conventional notions of culture and belonging. Alavi's practice often interrogates histories in the South West Asia and North Africa (SWANA) region, exploring their entanglements with globalization, settler colonialism, and the mobility and displacement of Black and Brown bodies.

DR JESSICA CLARK
lives and works on Wurundjeri Country VIC

Jessica Clark is a proud palawa/pallawah woman, born in lurtruwita/trouwerner and currently living and working on Wurundjeri Country in Naarm/Melbourne. She has a background in art history and art education and is currently Senior Curator, First Nations, at the National Gallery of Victoria. Her previous curatorial positions include Curator at the Australian Centre for Contemporary Art, 2022–25, and Curatorial Manager of the Victorian First Peoples Art and Design Fair at Creative Victoria, 2024–25. Jessica holds a PhD in Fine Art and Music, 2023, from the Victorian College of the Arts, University of Melbourne, for which she was awarded the Chancellor's Prize for Excellence in 2024. She is the current Ursula Hoff Fellow, 2024–26, at The University of Melbourne.

SARA M SALEH
lives and works on Gadigal Country NSW

Sara M Saleh is a writer/poet and human rights lawyer of Palestinian, Egyptian, and Lebanese heritage. Her debut novel, *Songs for the Dead and the Living, Affirm*, 2023, and her poetry collection, *The Flirtation of Girls*, UQP, 2023, have received multiple national and international prizes and shortlistings between them, and won the 2024 Barbara Jefferis Award and 2024 Anne Elder Award respectively. Rooted in the belief that literacy is a tool for liberation, Sara has rallied communities of artists across continents to create sustainable, generative, and inclusive spaces for craft, connection, and critical consciousness.

CURATOR BIOGRAPHY

DR NUR SHKEMBI OAM

lives and works on Wurundjeri Country VIC
born 1972, Christchurch, Aotearoa/New Zealand

Nur Shkembi is an award-winning curator, writer and art historian with a research specialisation in Islamic art history, contemporary art and postcolonial theory. Nur has produced and curated over 150 events, exhibitions and community engagement projects and was part of the core team which established the Islamic Museum of Australia. As a museum curator, Nur brought together artefacts, traditional art and contemporary art as a means for collective storytelling, subverting stereotypes and as a provision for the individual narrative. Nur is currently working on a new museum project in Western Sydney, due to open in 2028.

Exhibitions include *Soul Fury*, Bendigo Art Gallery, DOMINION Arts West Gallery, University of Melbourne and *Destiny Disrupted*, Griffith University Art Museum. Recent academic publications include 'Neo-Orientalism and the persistence of Holbein carpets: on writing the future history of Islamic art in Australia' in *What is postnational art history?*, Perimeter Editions and 'Destiny Disrupted: A History of Contemporary Islamic Art in 'Australia'' in *Variations*, Monash University Press. Nur holds a PhD in Art History from The University of Melbourne.

Acknowledgements

CURATOR ACKNOWLEDGEMENTS

I acknowledge the Wurundjeri Woi Wurrung people of the Kulin Nation as the traditional custodians of the lands and waterways where I live and work and pay my respects to their elders past and present. Sovereignty was never ceded.

It has been my great pleasure and honour to work with the extraordinary artists, contributors, and team at ACCA to deliver *Five Acts of Love*.

Firstly, I would like to thank the contributing artists, all of whom I wish to express my deepest gratitude for their contributions to the arts and society, as makers and storytellers who reflect, critique, guide, and truth tell through such immense beauty. I thank you for entrusting me with your work, it has been a great privilege: Abdul-Rahman Abdullah, Hoda Afshar, Megan Cope, Eugenia Flynn, D Harding, Saodat Ismailova, Khaled Sabsabi, Larissa Sansour & Søren Lind, Yhonnie Scarce, Ali Tahayori and Hossein Valamanesh.

Let's rewind a little, back to the beginning. My gratitude to former Artistic Director & CEO, Max Delany for reaching out in 2024 with the invitation to curate ACCA's 2025 winter season. Thank you for your belief in me and your support, guidance, generosity and enthusiasm for this project. Although my journey with ACCA did not begin with this project, I am so pleased to have been one of the final exhibitions on your ACCA dance card. My thanks are also extended to former Executive Director, Claire Richardson.

To the Board of Directors, I thank you for your unwavering support of *Five Acts of Love,* and for the bold vision you uphold for ACCA as the leading, experimental contemporary art centre in the country. And to ACCA's sponsors, supporters and friends, your continuing support of this excellent centre is a gift to us all.

I am greatly appreciative for the opportunity to work with Dr Jessica Clark and Dr Shelley McSpedden. Two brilliant curators, both Jess and Shelley have been instrumental in the development and delivery of the show. I am humbled to have such talent invested in my project. I am not sure if it's our shared (strange) love of art + footnotes that ultimately connects us, but here we are at the end of all this (no pun intended). Thank you for being the intelligent, brilliant and fierce women that you are.

A huge shout out to Senior Exhibitions Manager & Registrar extraordinaire Samantha Vawdrey and Exhibition Project Manager Shae Nagorcka. My question to you is simply this, how? HOW?! Hats off to you both.

Many thanks to the contributors of the publication for your talent, generosity and vulnerability: Dr Safdar Ahmed, Elyas Alavi, Dr Jessica Clark, Dr Eugenia Flynn and Sara M Saleh – and my thanks to Curator Sophie Prince and Designer Matt Hinkley for your publication expertise (and magic touch). And to publicist Katrina Hall, and the rest of the ACCA team, across education, marketing, visitor experience, installation, tech crews and volunteers. You are ALL brilliant. Thank you!

To the gallerists and collectors thank you for kindly facilitating and loaning artworks, Josh Milani (Milani Gallery, Meanjin/Brisbane), THIS IS NO FANTASY and Margaret Moore, as well as the Darebin Art Collection and team at Bundoora Homestead Art Centre. Special thanks to Angela Valamanesh and Nassiem Valamanesh for your commitment to this project and generous loan of Hossein's work. On this account, I would also like to extend my thanks to Professor Lisa Slade, Jane Devery and the Museum of Contemporary Art.

Finally, I extend my thanks to ACCA's recently appointed Artistic Director & CEO, Myles Russell-Cook. Thank you for your leadership, kindness and support.

To love is to risk everything.

ARTIST'S ACKNOWLEDGMENTS

Abdul-Rahman Abdullah would like to acknowledge the support of the Department of Local Government, Sports & Cultural Industries, WA, Moore Contempoary, Perth, Dr Nur Shkembi, the ACCA Team, and his family.

Megan Cope would like to acknowledge and thank the Quandamooka families who carry the legacy of fishing stories, the ancestors of Quandamooka kin dugongs, and Aimee Frodsham and Julie Skate from Canberra Glassworks.

D Harding would like to thank Josh Milani, Carol Vincent, Kyle McIntyre and Milani Gallery, Meanjin/Brisbane.

Saodat Ismailova's *Her right* 2020, is dedicated to all the brave women who were the first ones to unveil and go on stage, to act, dance, recite and empower other women to get education.

Ali Tahayori acknowledges his mother, Shahnaz, who left him the most precious legacy: a series of family photographs that became the *Archive of longing*. He also would like to thank his grandmother, Simin, who appears in many of the works, as well as the Parramatta Artists Studios on Dharug Land, where most of the works were created.

For the work of Hossein Valamanesh, gratitude is extended to Berenice Saliou and ICI, Paris, MCA, Sydney, and Tony Waite, Adelaide.

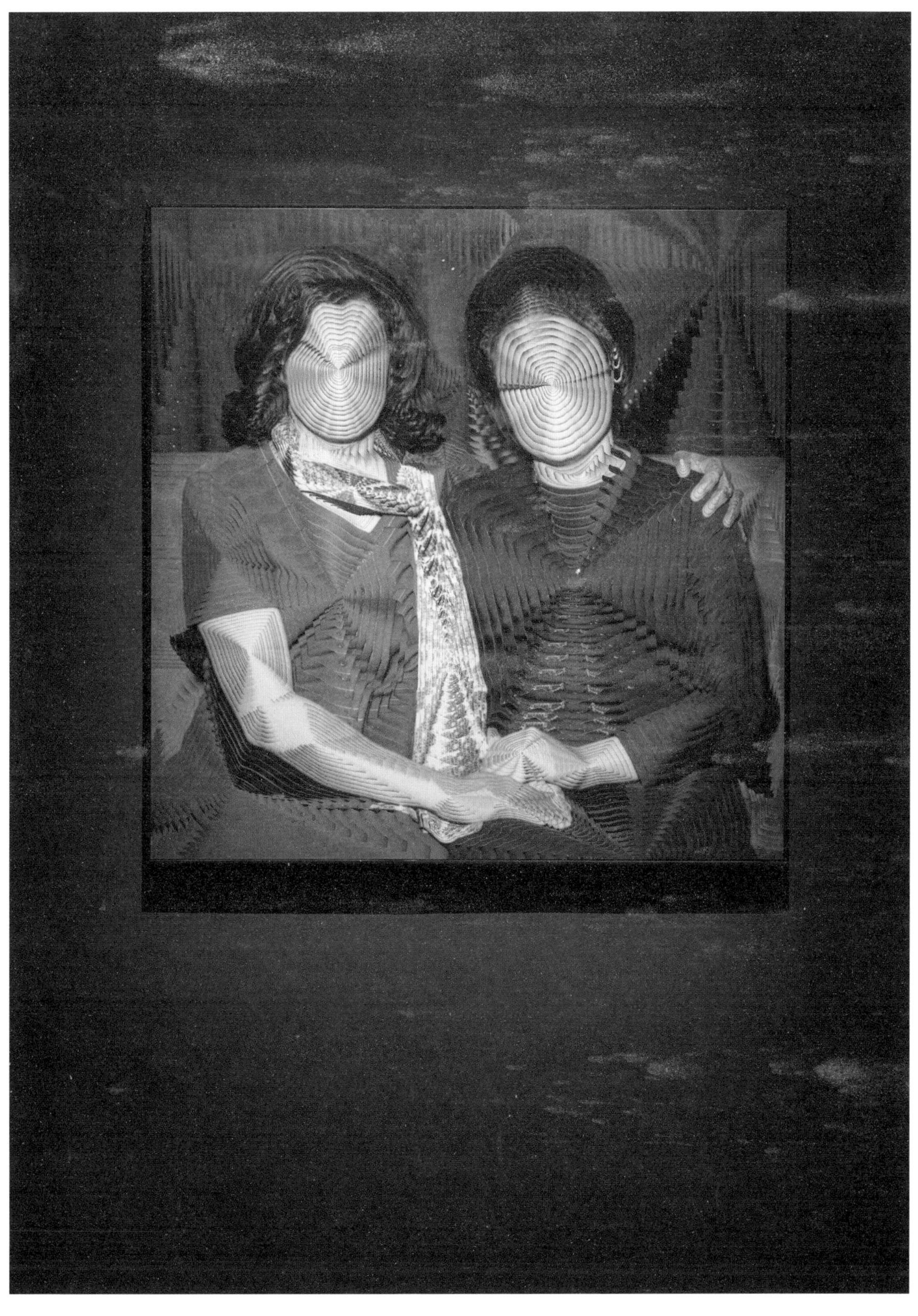

Ali Tahayori, *Sisterhood* 2021, pigment ink-jet print, collage,120.0 x 120.0 cm. Courtesy the artist and THIS IS NO FANTASY, Naarm/Melbourne

PROJECT CREDITS

Guest Curator
Dr Nur Shkembi OAM

Coordinating Curators
Jessica Clark
Shelley McSpedden

Senior Exhibitions Manager & Registrar
Samantha Vawdrey

Exhibition Project Manager
Shae Nagorcka

Editor
Dr Nur Shkembi OAM

Coordinating Editor & Copyeditor
Sophie Prince

Installation Team
Nicholas Currie
Nyx Mathews
Kurt Medenbach
Jacob Raupach
Nicholas Smith
Leon van de Graaff
Thomas Whelan

Dulux Paint Colours
Ticking

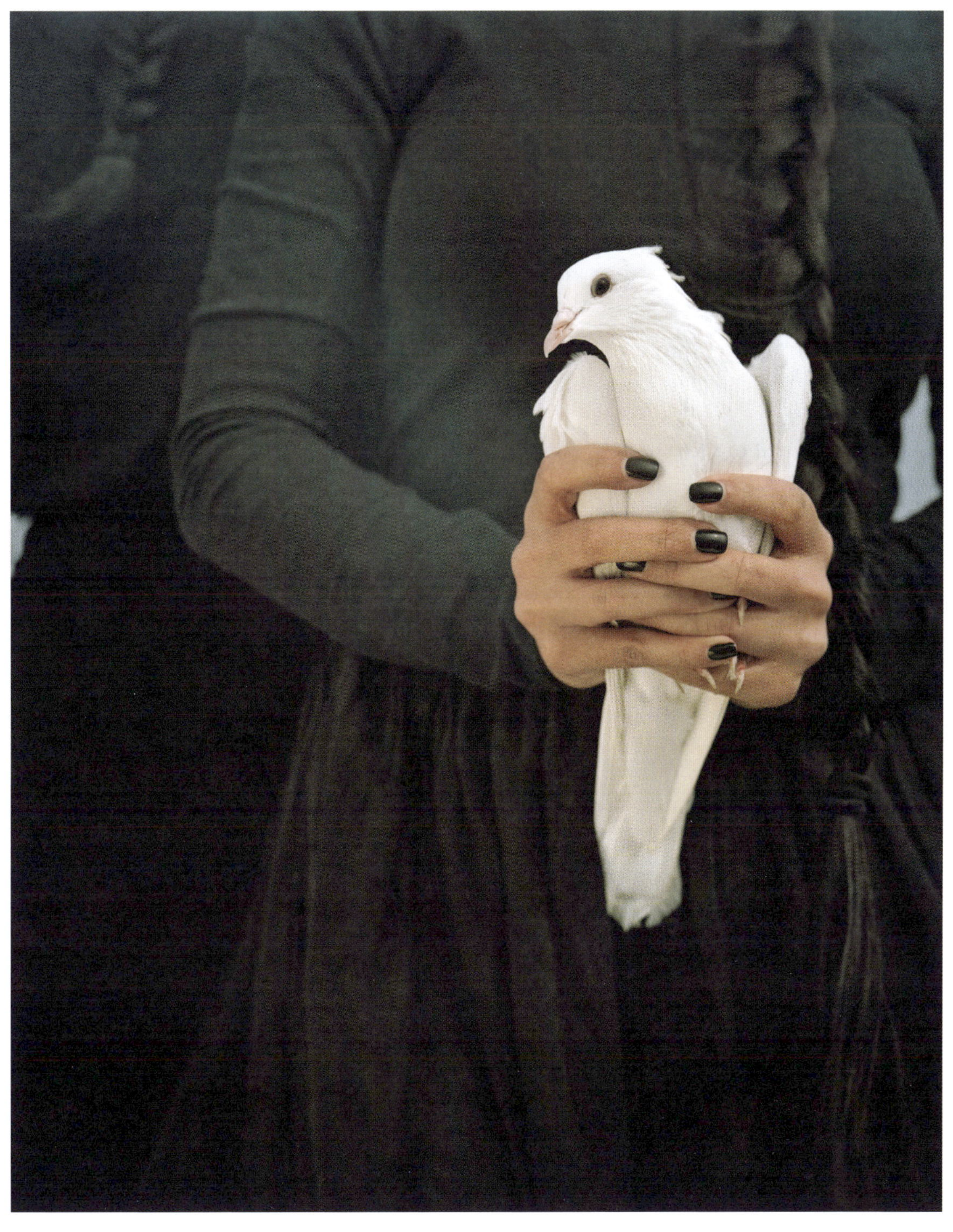

Hoda Afshar, *Untitled #7* from *In turn* series 2023, framed photographic print, 165.0 x 132.0 cm. Courtesy the artist and Milani Gallery, Meanjin/Brisbane

ACCA BOARD

Dr Terry Wu, Chair
Sarah Lynn Rees
Andrew Taylor
Gordon Thomson
John Tuck
Lisa Fox
Charlotte Day

Yalingwa Directions Circle
Aunty Joy Murphy Wandin AO (Chair)
Kylie Belling
Belinda Briggs
Hetti Perkins
Stacie Piper
Hannah Presley

Associate Elders
N'arweet Carolyn Briggs AM

ACCA STAFF

Myles Russell-Cook
Artistic Director & CEO

Laura De Neefe
Director, Development & Engagement

Sari DeMallory
Senior Development & Engagement Manager

Dr Shelley McSpedden
Senior Curator and Head of Exhibitions

Sophie Prince
Curator

Samantha Vawdrey
Senior Exhibitions Manager & Registrar

Shae Nagorcka
Exhibitions Project Manager

Mark Hislop
Operations Manager

Felicia Pinchen-Hogg
Head of Learning & Creative Engagement

Minna Lappalainen
Education & Access Coordinator

Lauren Simmonds
Artist Educator

Freya Alexander
Education & Creative Engagement Coordinator

Xuan Wei Yap
Development & Marketing Coordinator

Alice Fairweather
Executive Grants & Marketing Coordinator

Badra Aji
Senior Visitor Experience Manager

Bridget Thompson
Digital Engagement Strategist & Producer

Maggie Lu
Accounts Coordinator

Matt Hinkley
Designer

Katrina Hall
Publicist

ACCA Educators
Suzannah Griffith
Mimmalisa Trifilo
Te Maia Williams
Charlie Farmer

Visitor Experience Coordinators
Jasmine Babayan
Arini Byng
Ponie Curtis
Katinka Samuel
Dom Viggiani
Beatriz Airah Yu

Visitor Experience Team
Suzannah Griffith
Jacinta Maude
Leah Nathan
Beatrice Rubio-Gabriel

Volunteers
Olivia Acciarito
Prudence Anderson
Sophia Armstrong
Alanna Baxter
Lily Baxter
Billee Byrne
Nommy Cai
Maeve Carpenter
Mi-Chieh Chen
Lara Cutajar
Aisyah Kirana Fardiansyah
Daisy Giuffrida
Aisha Hara
Talita Indriagustry
Bambi Johnson
Minadi Gajaman Kankanamge
Jodi Kashani
Eugenie Gullifer-Laurie
Giulia Lallo
Krystal Shihan Liu
Qing Liu
Ebony Maurice-Wilmott
Sarah McArthur
Cooper Motley
Mauliandini Nur Noviasri
Hina Omukai
Xinxin Ouyang
Theodora Pantelich
Sienna Pavlovski
Linh Pham
Emily Prater
Pearl Reilly-Murray
Kira Richards
Lewellyn Riley-Haynes
Litani Risty
Candice Savira
Faith Seci
Nadja Slovák
Olivia Smyth
Emily Song
Daniel Song
Amelia Spencer
CJ Starc
Jeanne Kartika Tanujaya
Fernanda Ureta
Grace Vescovi
Catherine Weng
Anna (Yuqing) Xiang
Sheung Yi Sharon Yau
Joshua Yong

ACCA DONORS

VISIONARY
Lisa Fox, Vivien & Graham Knowles, Bruce Parncutt AO, Drs Theresia & Kevin Spencer

LEGEND
Dr Terry Wu & Lucinda Tee-Wu, Patagorang Foundation

CHAMPION
D'Lan Contemporary, McNiven & Russell Research Fund

GUARDIAN
Wendy & Paul Bonnici and Family, Thomas Bridge, Rosemary Forbes & Ian Hocking, Rob Gould Foundation, Michael Schwarz & David Clouston, Craig Semple, Frank Pollio, Rosemary Walls, Watts Family

PATRON
Sam & Tania Brougham, Paul & Samantha Cross, Georgia Dacakis, Andy Dinan & Mario Lo Giudice, Troy Emery, Linda Herd, Joanna Horgan & Peter Wetenhall, Katja Mouvlin & Travis John Ficarra, Marita Onn & John Tuck, Ursula Sullivan & Joanna Strumpf, Rob Watson & Bryan Carroll

FRIEND
Lesley Alway & Paul Hewison, Tony Albert, Paul Auckett, Professor Andrew Benjamin, Kyle Czech & Peter Buffett, Dr Sue Dodd, Elly Fink, Fiona, Emily Floyd, Jane & Simon Hayman, Jane Hemstritch AO, I and T Henderson Foundation, Kosloff Architecture, Elizabeth Leslie, Mark McMahon & Rita Zhang, Keryn & Stephen Nossal, A/Prof., Drew Pettifer & Thomas Lloyde, Jane Ryan & Nick Kharsas, Somage, Jennifer Strauss AM, Patricia Szonert, Noel & Jenny Turnbull, Cavan Wee | W Private

CONTEMPORARY
Katrina Sedgwick, Vida Gaigalas & Chris Barker

ENTHUSIAST
Bigbamboo, Rachel Bernhaut, Julia Gardiner, Peta Heffernan, Melbourne Homeschool Collective, Myra

The Australian Centre for Contemporary Art gratefully acknowledges the bequest intention of Roger Chao, whose future gift will support the next generation of artists. We also extend our heartfelt thanks to all donors who choose to remain anonymous.

ACCA PARTNERS AND SUPPORTERS

Government Partners

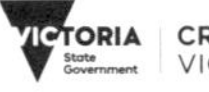

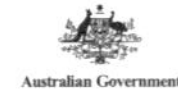

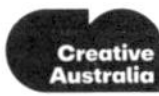

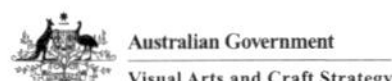

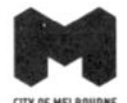

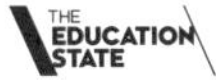

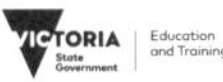

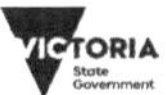

Partners

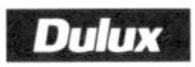

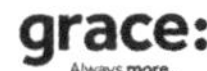

SUPERNORMAL
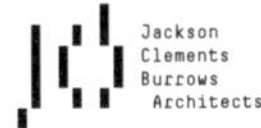

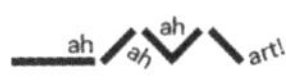

TABOO
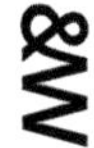
Fish · Nankivell

Trusts and Foundations

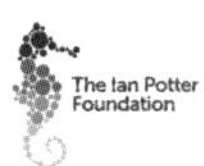

Media Partners

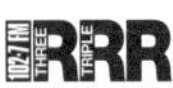

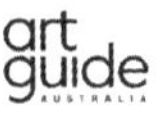

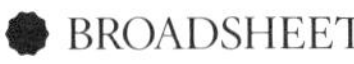

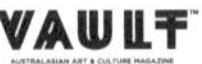

Event Partners

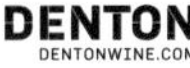

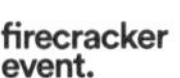

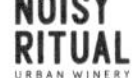

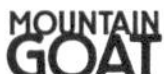

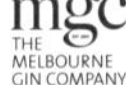

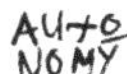

MAiDENii
VERMOUTH

THE
GOSPEL
RYE WHISKEY
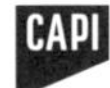

Supporters

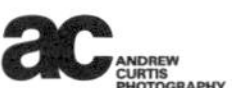

Network Partners

CONTEMPORARY
ARTS
ORGANISATIONS
AUSTRALIA

FIVE ACTS OF LOVE

Australian Centre for Contemporary Art

27 June – 24 August 2025

Curator: Dr Nur Shkembi OAM

Published 2025

ISBN: 978-0-6458328-7-7

Australian Centre for Contemporary Art
111 Sturt Street
Southbank VIC 3006
Melbourne, Australia
acca.melbourne

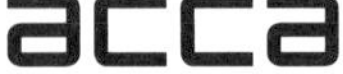

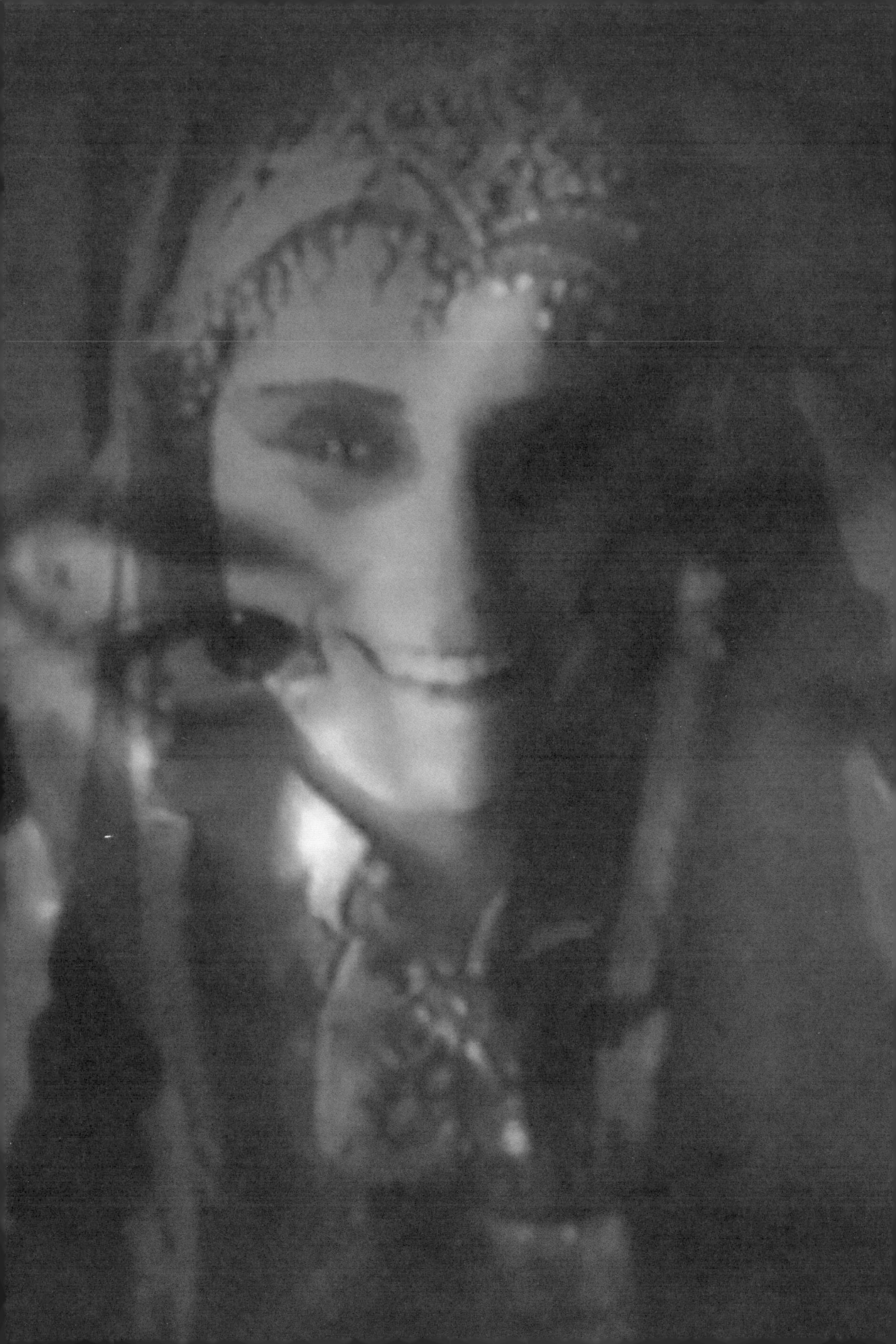

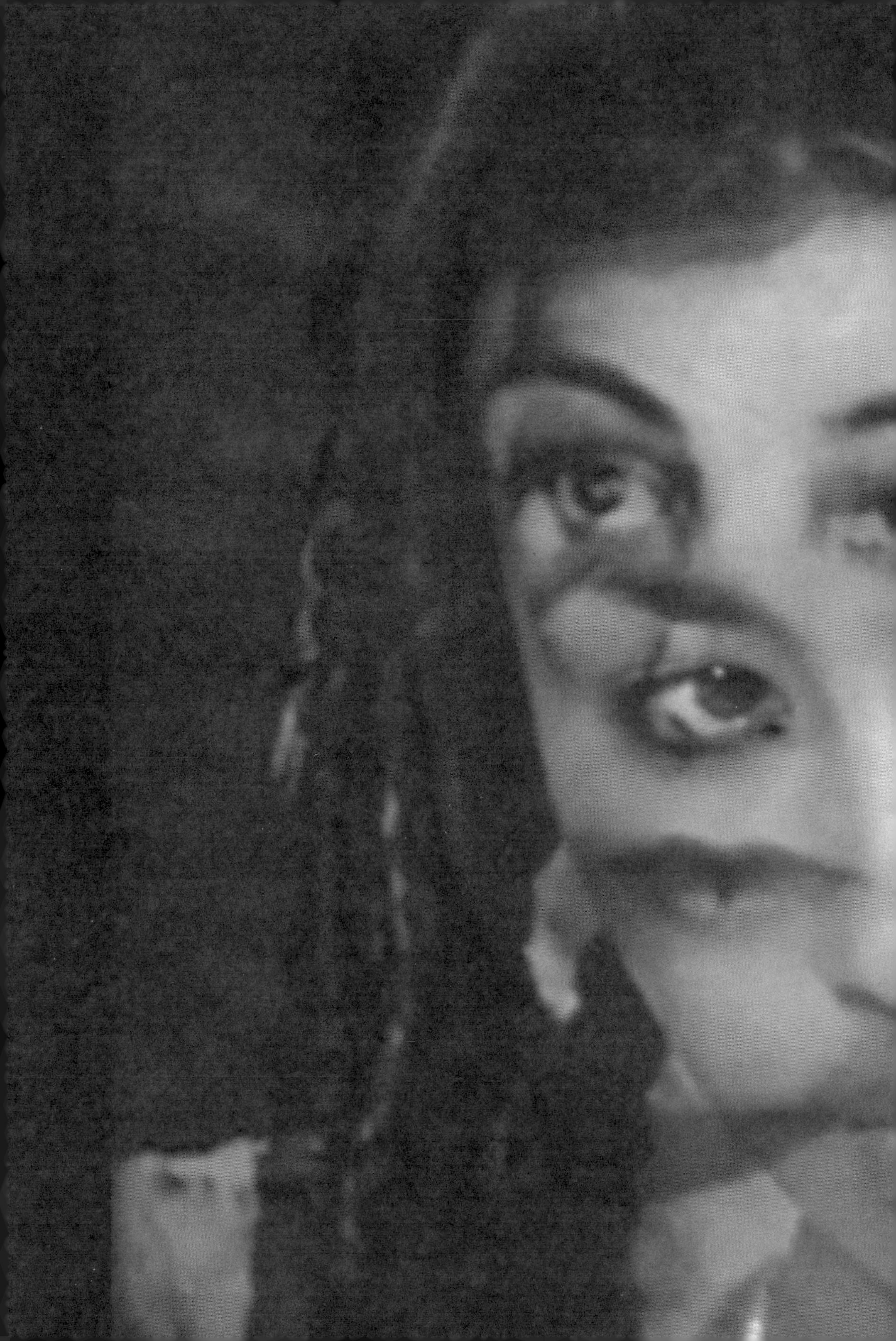